OTZ CHIM

FOUNDATIONS OF PRACTICAL SORCERY VOLUME V

FOUNDATIONS OF PRACTICAL SORCERY VOLUME V

OTZ CHIM

THE TREE OF LIFE

Gary St. M. Nottingham

Published by Avalonia
www.avaloniabooks.co.uk

Published by Avalonia

BM Avalonia
London
WC1N 3XX
England, UK
www.avaloniabooks.co.uk

OTZ CHIM
Copyright © 2012 G. St. M. Nottingham

First Edition 2012.
This revised edition, 2015.

All rights reserved.

ISBN 978-1-905297-78-8

Design by Satori, for Avalonia.

British Library Cataloguing in Publication Data. A catalogue record for this book is available from the British Library.

All rights reserved. No part of this publication may be reproduced or utilised in any form or by any means, electronic or mechanical, including photocopying, microfilm, recording, or by any information storage and retrieval system, or used in another book, without written permission from the author.

About the Author

Gary St. M. Nottingham's commitment to the study and practice of the alchemical arte, ritual magic, grimoires and spirit conjuration means that he can often be found peering at bubbling flasks or a shewstone – or otherwise engaged in deepening his knowledge and understanding of such matters. His practices also draw on the work of the 17th-century astrologer William Lilly and the arte of horary astrology.

He organised the legendary Ludlow Esoteric Conference (2004-2008), helped produce Verdelet occult magazine, has taught many free day workshops on basic occult skills and is a popular speaker at esoteric conferences.

The seven volumes of Foundations of Practical Sorcery are an unabridged collection of Gary's much sought-after previously published work, updated and made available to a wider readership at last.

Gary was raised in south Shropshire, where, during his mid-teens, he became involved with a small Coven, thereby gaining an excellent grounding in a wide selection of magical practices. Following the conjuration of a spirit, and asking it for help that manifested when least expected, he subsequently became involved with a group of practising alchemists. He has a background in horticulture, enjoys spending time in the garden and playing chess.

And the Lord God said,
'Behold the Man has become as one of us, To know good and evil:
And now, lest he put forth his hand and take also of The Tree of Life
And eat and live forever.'

    (*Genesis* 3:22)

Table of Contents

INTRODUCTION 8

'OUT OF NOTHING CAME ALL' 11
'APPROACHING THE LADDER OF LIGHT' 16
'THE TEN STATIONS OF DESCENDING LIGHT' 21
'THE PATHS OF THE TREE' 47
PRAXIS - THE WORK 97
RITES AND RITUALS 107

FURTHER READING 119
INDEX 121

Introduction

We live in an age where we are awash with information on all subjects, and to this the magical artes are no exception. Whilst the student of magic can easily access all manner of electronic files there is nothing quite like a book.

A book can not only be picked up and read, but will, in many instances, over time, become a friend, guide and teacher who has assisted the reader on their journey throughout their life. Quite simply books can change lives and this is why those who have been in positions of power through the centuries have tried, and often failed, to keep knowledge out of the hands of everyday folk. This is perhaps primarily because they feared the power of the book to cause change, and change is what the seven books in the Foundations of Practical Sorcery series will cause.

Today the magical artes have never been so accessible, although that doesn't mean the demands that the arte makes upon the practitioner have been lessened in any way. While the arte is, in principle, for all, not everyone will have the self-discipline, the will and the imagination to succeed therein. However for those who do have these basic attributes or are prepared to acquire them there is much to be gained from the practice of magic in all levels of life. For many people their ingress into the arte will be by books, and the exploration of and working with the information they contain. There is nothing like experience even if your magic proves less successful than hoped for: there is no such thing as failure in magic, because every experience will, at the very least, teach the practitioner something, even if it's just to try harder next time!

Of course some will have access to a magical group and the knowledge and collective experience to be found therein; but for many this will not be the case. Magical groups regardless of hue by and large have much to commend them, but not all of them do. I have in the past been approached by people who have gone through a coven system yet then been led to ask me to help them practice and study magic. It seemed their coven did not in fact practice the arte; which left me wondering what was it that they did do. I am aware of similar approaches made to other magical practitioners, which has left me concluding that some magical groups and covens can actually be detrimental to an individual's magical development and understanding - although this is certainly not the case with all by any means.

Foundations of Practical Sorcery goes some way to rectifying this deficit in any student's magical life. They offer clear magical instruction and accounts of magical acts to be performed, thus making the arte easily accessible. The methods and techniques presented are all based upon my own personal knowledge and experience which goes back over forty years, methods and techniques that have worked successfully for me and will do so for any reader who applies them accordingly.

In many ways I was fortunate, during the autumn of 1972, to meet a magical practitioner who taught me much regarding the arte, generously affording me the run of their magical library as well. Having been schooled extensively in magical knowledge from my mid teen years I consider myself to have been extremely fortunate and lucky to have had many experiences not easily available to many people. Thus the present Foundations of Practical Sorcery series is the distillation of four decades of successful magical workings.

Each of the seven volumes gives a clear account and rendition of one or another area of magical instruction that I have received and have been taught. They are presented to the reader in a clear and workable style which will provide them with a concise and firm foundation, allowing the serious magical student to explore the Western Magical Tradition, the inheritance of us all.

Gary St. M. Nottingham, February 2015

Gary St. M. Nottingham

CHAPTER ONE

'Out of Nothing Came All'

The Holy Kabbalah has a long history and has been highly influential on the Western Magical Traditions. Whilst it is expressed through the Judaic traditions and the use of Judaic concepts are apparent, it must be remembered that the Jewish culture came originally from the *'Fertile Crescent'* - that land rich in heritage that lies between the rivers Euphrates and the Tigris. The home to much of the development of man and civilization.

Yet arising in the cultures that grew in this area was the concept of Inanna the Great Goddess who had a sacred garden wherein grew the *'Tree of Knowledge'* which was guarded by a serpent. To me this story suggests that the biblical story of the Garden of Eden and the tree thereof is a story from this culture, which the Jews left as they looked for their own sacred lands in which to settle.

With this exodus they would have taken with them the religious stories and concepts that they had experienced, subsequently they developed their own religion but re-wrote some of the stories to fit with their new religious concepts. Stories such as the flood and of course the Tree in the Garden of Eden are but two. For me, the story of the Tree is an old story, one that is older than both the Christian and Jewish cultures and goes back to the birth and rise of mankind in the Fertile Crescent.

The Tree of Life is one of the most important symbols in Western magic, it shows the relationship between the powers that form creation and their manifestation within mankind and all that exists. Regardless of whether it manifests at this level of being or another; everything is interrelated. Thus, that which is above is like that which is below. To have an effect on one will grant an effect on the other. Therefore with the development of the powers of concentration and visualisation, and also the creation of forms, they can by the use of will-power be ensouled by higher forces and driven down the planes to manifest at the everyday levels, be it internal or external to the individual who is summoning them.

This is magic and the magical use of the Holy Kabbalah. And yet there is more: with the use of Kabbalistic concepts and symbolism in magic such as imagery and sounds, the Kabbalist can experience the mystical exploration of creation via various meditative praxes. This is a more reflective mode of working than using ritual magic, which requires more training. This work will help prepare the student of the arte. Traditionally the Holy Kabbalah has been an oral tradition, passing via mouth to ear to the student, and was never written down until the thirteenth century. Being an important part of the Western Magical Traditions the study and practice of it will prepare the student for the study of Western Magic as its symbology becomes part of the warp and weft of the individual's soul.

The Kabbalah says that originally creation came out of nothing, and that nothing concentrated itself to a point and became something. To do this, something must have existed with a consciousness to realise this? The Kabbalistic text the *Zohar* says that, *'Before having created any shape in the world, before having produced any form, He was alone, without form, resembling nothing. Who could comprehend Him as He then was, before creation, since he had no form?'*

This is an incomprehensible state, unknown and unknowable by our human consciousness, and is part of *'God's Mystery.'* Of this primal reality all speculation is futile as the mystery is simply beyond humanity at this stage of being. Yet it is from this state that all creation flows and to which all creation returns and therefore everything that exists, has existed, or will exist, is but an expression of this truth, whether one denies it or not, for it has and always will be. All life is, regardless of this, wherever or whenever, however lowly or exalted, whether animal, mineral or vegetable, an expression of God and is alive at its own level; full of this Holy Mystery should we but appreciate it. The *Zohar* says that from Kether, the Crown, descends this holy power through all levels to Malkuth, our everyday world, and that by doing so all that exists is sustained. By the use of regular meditative and devotional endeavour we will implant the roots of this Holy Tree within our consciousness where it will bear such fruits as higher spiritual perceptions and an increase in psychic sensitivities, as well as a glimpse of divinity and the workings thereof.

The Kabbalah considers that the Holy Tree, with its twenty-two paths and ten Sephiroth, form what is called Adam Kadmon, the Heavenly Man. The ten Sephiroth, which are interlinked with the twenty-two paths, are the cosmic principles that are the Macrocosm, the Greater Creation. This in turn is reflected within Man, who contains all the principles, but on a smaller scale, the Microcosm. Thus Man is made in the image of God and by understanding our own natures can the created comprehend the Creator.

As the *Sepher ha Zohar* claims,

> 'That which constitutes the real man is the soul, and those things which are called the skin, the flesh, the bones and the veins, - all these are merely a veil, an outward covering, but not the man himself. When a man departs, he divests himself of all these garments wherewith he is clothed. Yet all these bones and sinews and the different parts of the body are formed in the secrets of divine wisdom after the heavenly image. The skin typifies the heavens that are infinite in extent, covering all things as a garment. The bones and the veins symbolise the divine chariot, the inner powers of Man. But these are the outer garments, for in the inward part is the deep mystery of the Heavenly Man.'

Imbued within this is consciousness, which, with the faculties of emotion and intellect, allows us to explore and experience creation at all levels and indeed express our own natures for good or for ill. This allows Man the opportunity to develop a higher consciousness with which he can gain the Attainment with God, the goal of all mystical systems regardless of their culture or place in human history.

The Kabbalah makes clear that the tree is expressed via the Four Worlds of Atziluth, Briah, Yetzirah and Assiah.

Atziluth:

י

Hebrew ,letter Yod. Spirit, that which connects with God. Within man these principles relate to the following:

Yechidah - the pure spirit which connects with God.

Chiah - the creative will or impulse.

Neschamah - intuition or the understanding of the will.

Briah:

Hebrew letter Heh, Creation, the world of archangelic concepts. Here the principle of the Ruach is expressed, the intellect. It is also the ego, which has been developed by the Higher Self, the Yechidah, to become aware of that which has been created as it desires things and tries to attain them as it explores the worlds around it. It contains perceptions, sensations, thoughts, emotions and desires. Also this is where memory, will, imagination, desire and reason abound. All these drive our everyday thoughts which need to be harnessed to *'the work.'*

Yetzirah:

ו

Hebrew letter Vav, the worlds of formation, angelic. At this level the Nephesch is expressed, which is the grosser side of the spirit and is the cravings of the instincts for the physicality of life. But that is not all for also at this level are the etheric levels of man and creation within which flow the subtle forces that vivify life. Also known as Chi or Prana, also the secret fire of alchemy, the life force. This is the level of the astral body of man and all that is created. It is at these levels that magic needs to take place to effect the physical levels.

Assiah:

Hebrew letter Heh, (final), the physical world of action and experience, elemental spirits and man. Where the animal body is known as The Guph. The lower self who needs to be disciplined and brought under the will of the higher self. Its constant demand for attention and the fulfillment of its chattering desires are endless and takes up a lot of emotional and mental energy which can be better used at a higher level. Thus the body must be made to serve the higher and is but a servant, a means to explore life at this level. With its constant cries for attention and fulfillment of every changing desire it is not the master. *'It is the beast whereon he rideth.'*

Therefore the true object of magic can be seen as the return of Man to God, that is, the uniting of the individual's consciousness during one's life with the greater consciousness of creation, the source of all light, life and love. Only thus can true understanding, liberty and knowledge be granted to see the beauty, majesty and power of life. As the flower opens and faces the sun to imbibe the forces of life, so must the Kabbalist open and draw upon their own spiritual self. Therefore by discovering their inner self and the forming of an indissoluble relationship with God and the powers of creation, the Kabbalist can then find the answers to life's problems and their own place in the great game of life.

'For the knowledge of God is accomplished by a knowledge of ourselves.'

CHAPTER TWO

'Approaching the Ladder of Light'

The Tree of Life is represented as ten stations of descending light that originate with the creator. Each of these stations, which are called Sephiroth (Sephira, singular), is a cosmic principle and is approached through colour, imagery and sound. They are linked to one another by twenty-two paths, which are represented by the twenty-two letters of the Hebrew alphabet. Beyond the spheres of the Tree is the limitless light, the Ain Soph. This is beyond the comprehension of mankind at this level and that is all that can be said of it.

However by meditation and with the use of ritual the powers of the Tree can be explored and experienced. Insights into the human condition can be granted as well as the solutions to problems: sometimes that which has been experienced or the symbolism that appears in a meditation on some aspect of the Tree can appear in everyday life during the following few days or in dreams, very much like Jung's concepts of synchronicity or meaningful coincidence.

The spheres are placed on three pillars; the right-hand pillar is male and deemed to be mercy, whilst the left-hand pillar is female and is severity, with the middle pillar being the point of stability between the two extremes.

All the paths and Sephiroth are expressed through the four worlds of the Kabbalah within which they all interact causing all that happens in the world and how man then reacts to them. This can be seen in *Isaiah* 45:7 where God declares that he is responsible for all that is both good and bad that happens in the world.

However the question arises, if God is *'All Powerful'* why doesn't he stop bad things from happening? If by the same token he is all good why do bad things happen? Perhaps God is not *'All Powerful nor All*

Good?' Unless bad things are meant to happen, and mankind is tested in the quality of their character and is given the opportunity to develop spiritual awareness by experiencing the sufferings through which they are going through? If this is not the case then we must accept that there is no God or that God is not All Powerful or indeed All Good.

Kabbalah teaches that there is a big plan and that we are an important part of it as it is expressed through our natures and the way that we react to events. Therefore evil can become a potency that promotes good as we try to combat it thus restoring balance; the lesson of the middle pillar. Again the question arises, when does mercy become weakness and firmness become cruelty? Such speculation is all very well when one is safe, well-fed and warm, but not if one is cold, wet and homeless, with no one to care or indeed help.

The Kabbalah teaches that mankind was originally before the Throne of God, but fell into matter so that the Divine Will could be expressed. Mankind, created in the image of God and bearing within their being part of that divinity is raised above and set apart from the rest of creation - angelic, demonic and that which is here on middle earth.

This is the mystery of Daath the Sephira which is but a shadow on the Tree below Kether, the Crown. Sadly most of humanity are asleep to their own spirituality.

Within the Kabbalah is the concept of the Shekinah, the female aspect of the creator. Sometimes she is seen as the World Spirit, or in some Kabbalistic schools as the Divine Bride of God from which all creation flows. Others consider her to be the Christian concept of the Holy Spirit, the indwelling divine spark within mankind. *Proverbs* 3:17-18 makes it quite clear that:

> 'Her ways are of pleasantness and her paths are peace… and happy is everyone that retaineth her.'

Attributes:

The way that symbolism is applied and interpreted is a major key to Kabbalistic praxis, and it is worth considering the attributes of the symbols and the interplay between them. Not only are colours associated with each of the Sephira (singular) Sephiroth (plural) but so are names, incense, imagery and text. All this will be explored accordingly as they are an important aspect of the modus operandi of the Holy Kabbalah and are keys to meditative and visionary states that can be experienced with this spiritual discipline. Symbols are keys that speak to the deeper parts of the psyche and beyond, especially when empowered by the emotions that can be generated by sacred drama. Ceremonial magic is an art form as much as a spiritual discipline, that can uplift and inspire the soul.

God Names:

These are associated with each of the Sephiroth and are the names which are aspects of the highest and therefore belong to the Atziluth aspect of the Sephira. One must appreciate that all God Names are aspects of the One Creative Spirit. These are used as keys to engage with the energies that they represent.

Magical Imagery:

The use of imagery over centuries builds around it a reservoir of energy which can be tapped and used magically. The image will represent a concept or state, we can see this every day with advertising promoting imagery which will automatically suggest that which the advertiser wishes you to accept; this is also done with politics and religion on a regular basis. The imagery associated with the Sephira and the use of the God Name becomes a potent point of ingress to the mysteries of each Sephira.

Archangel:

Angel originally meant messenger which gives something of its function. The archangel is seen as the being that is responsible for organising the work of each of the Sephira and is always invoked in the God Name of the relevant Sephira. Each archangel will be seen in the colours of the Sephira which it is associated with. The name of the archangel will end in EL which denotes that it is a winged being from God and is therefore holy. The forms of the archangels are built by man as symbols that represent them but indwelling is a potency that is real and can be experienced. Archangels belong to the world of Briah or creative force.

Angelic Orders:

The angels of the Sephiroth belong to the worlds of Yetzirah or the formative worlds. These beings are worked with after the invocation of the God Name of the relevant Sephira and then the archangelic being. Included within the Orders of Angels are such spiritual creatures as nature spirits and elementals. Some angels will work with the destiny of a nation or a group of people and also with animals or plants. Some angels become the *genius loci* of a place, such as a valley or a hill. Communication with them tends to be more subconscious and the ideas that they convey will be impressed upon the recipient's conscious mind via their subconscious. Whilst angels are powerful in their own realms they do not have mankind's spiritual potential as only man has eaten of the Tree of the Knowledge of Good and Evil, thus granting him the potentiality of God.

Mundane Chakra:

This is the planet that is seen as the manifestation of the energy of the Sephira at the level of Assiah.

Yetziratic Texts:

These are traditional texts that help to describe each of the Sephiroth and the connecting paths. They are drawn from an early Kabbalistic text known as *Sepher Yetzirah* or the *Book of Formation*. Despite the obscure language they are useful to suggest the potencies that they represent to the subconscious mind.

Spiritual Experience:

Sometimes called the Vision, meaning the granting of a state of mind that expresses the potencies of the Sephira from which it originates. It will explain something of its powers and grant a glimpse of the workings of divinity.

Virtue & Vice:

These are considered to be the reactions of the psyche to the forces of the Sephira. The virtue of the Sephira is that which is conferred whilst the vice is the result of an imbalance caused by weakness within the human psyche.

Symbols:

These are meditative keys that can help to access the potencies of each Sephira. As the subconscious mind can be communicated with through the use of symbols and emotion, these become the language thereof and the symbols of each Sephira will be found useful in this action.

Colours and Incense:

These are important to the construction of rites and rituals that relate to each of the Sephira and will often appear in some way during meditations and pathworkings as keys to the experience.

Tarot Card:

The twenty-two tarot trumps are associated with the twenty-two letters of the Hebrew alphabet and can be used as access points during meditation on the paths. This is a far cry from the populist fortune-telling that they are generally associated with.

CHAPTER THREE

'The Ten Stations of Descending Light'

Kether:

'The First Path is called the Admirable or Hidden Intelligence because it is the light giving the power of comprehension of the First Principle which hath no beginning. And it is the primal glory because no created being can attain its essence.'

Titles:	The Crown. The Vast Countenance. Concealed of Concealed.
Magical Imagery:	A Bearded King who is seen in profile.
God Name:	Ehieh, meaning *'I Am.'*
Archangel:	Metatron. Angel of the Divine Presence.
Angelic Orders:	Chaioth ha Qadesh. Holy Living Creatures.
Mundane Chakra:	Primum Mobile. The First Swirlings. Rashith ha Gilgalim.
Spiritual Experience:	Union with God.
Virtue:	Completion of the Great Work.
Vice:	None
Symbols:	A Crown. The Point. The Swastika.
Incense:	Ambergris.

Colour in Atziluth:	Brilliance.
Colour in Briah:	Pure White Brilliance.
Colour in Yetzirah:	Pure White Brilliance.
Colour in Assiah:	White flecked gold.

Kether is the first manifestation which came into being from the Great Unmanifest. It contains the potential of all things, and from Kether flows all manifestation, and unto Kether everything does return. It is positioned at the head of the Holy Tree and is pure spirit at its highest attribution. The God Name meaning *'I Am'* is all that can be said about Kether at this stage of human evolution as its mysteries are beyond comprehension, yet sometimes we can get a glimpse of its mystery. Its colours which are brilliance and white encompass all other colours; this is pertinent as all creation flows from Kether thus all the other colours can be found within its being.

Archangel:

The Archangel of Kether is Metatron who made the knowledge of the Kabbalah accessible to mankind, he is often contemplated as a pillar of brilliant light. The name is from the Greek and comes from *Meta Ton Thronos*, meaning *'Near thy Throne.'* He is seen as the being who mediates at the highest level between the Creator and the Created.

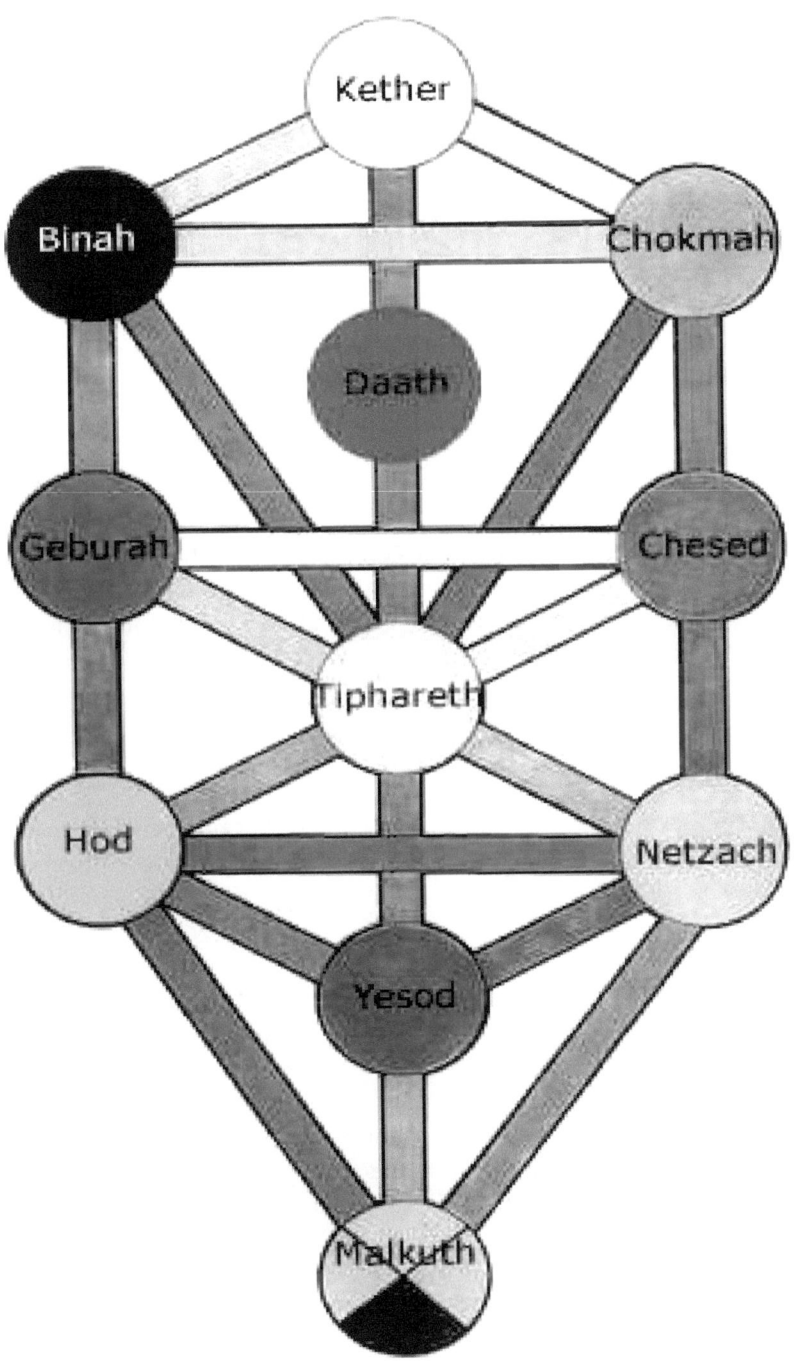

Angelic Orders:

These are the four Holy Living Creatures who are depicted as the Bull, Lion, Eagle and Man. They are often seen as the four gospels of Christianity, however they are associated with the four elements; Bull – earth, Lion – fire, Eagle – water, Man – air; these symbols are the fixed astrological signs of Taurus, Leo, Scorpio and Aquarius. They are also expressed via the aces of the Tarot and represent the elemental powers pentacles, wands, cups and swords. These elements are principles and aspects of God and by meditating on their symbology we can grasp something of the nature of divinity. They can also be experienced by way of the four Jungian psychological functions of sensations (earth), intellect (fire), feeling (water) and intuition (air).

Mundane Chakra:

This is the Primum Mobile or the First Swirlings, which is seen as a spinning swastika (an Eastern symbol used within Judaic mysteries, ironically abused by Hitler and the Nazi party). This symbol can be used with the four Holy Living Creatures seen at each of its four arms and spinning as it is absorbed by one's consciousness and experienced in meditation.

Virtue:

The Completion of the Great Work or the Union of Man with God is rather self-explanatory and is the goal of all mystical systems regardless of symbolism. This is also the spiritual experience. At this level there can be no vice.

Colour:

The colours which are given relate to the four levels of creation and are therefore to be used at the level to which they relate. For example, if contemplating the Assiah levels of Kether then the colours given, which are white flecked gold, would be used to build up in the mind the symbols that are associated with Kether at this level. Therefore the spinning swastika as a symbol of Kether at this level would be visualised in white flecked gold. Symbols and colours are important at this level as they speak to the deeps of the mind.

Chokmah:

'The second path is called the Illuminating Intelligence. It is the crown of creation, the splendour of unity, equalling it. It is exalted over every head and is named the second glory.'

Titles:	Supernal Father. Sky Father. Wisdom. Yod.
Magical Imagery:	A bearded male figure.
God Name:	YHVH, meaning *'Lord.'*
Archangel:	Ratziel. The Herald of God.
Angelic Orders:	Auphanim. The Encirclers. The Wheels.
Mundane Chakra:	Masloth. The Sphere of the Zodiac.
Spiritual Experience:	The Vision of God Face to Face.
Virtue:	Devotion.
Vice:	None
Symbols:	The phallus. Standing stone. Straight line. Uplifted rod of power. The tower and mountain top.
Incense:	Musk.
Colour in Atziluth:	Soft Blue.
Colour in Briah:	Slate grey.
Colour in Yetzirah:	Pearl grey.
Colour in Assiah:	White flecked red, blue and yellow.

Chokmah, meaning wisdom, is the second Sephira on the Tree of Life. It is the divine driving force that manifests throughout creation and is considered to be masculine. In a passive manner it is a reflection of the out-pouring force of Kether. It is considered that Kether, which manifested out of nothing, was alone and self-created. Upon self-reflection a self image is created and this imagery then takes on an objective existence, the first projection from which all creation then proceeds. Therefore Chokmah is seen as the Crown of Creation and is *'exalted above every head.'* Being male Chokmah is seen as the *'All Father,'* the source of all male sexuality. On an esoteric level sexuality is seen as an expression of the life force within a person. If the life force is blocked off at some level it will seek to express its nature at another level thus creating neurosis and problems.

Whilst sexual instincts are a means for the life force to express itself the sexual act is a function not a force. It is this life force, the life force of God, which is of the nature of Chokmah and is holy. Yet sadly, in the West, the sanctity of sexuality is not appreciated, which is why it doesn't appear in religious arte where it should do - because what could be more holy than the life force and the creation of life that it grants?

Archangel:

The archangel of Chokmah is Ratziel, *'The Herald of God.'* A title that is self-explanatory as this is the first of the holy Sephira from which all things in creation flow. It is from this archangel that the concept and gaining of wisdom flows.

Angelic Orders:

The Auphanim are the angels of Chokmah and are the forces of motion expressed in their name meaning *'Wheels.'* Thus they are responsible for the movement within creation as without them all things would be static and there would be no movement, no cycle of events and no evolution of man's spirit.

Mundane Chakra:

This is the Zodiac, the circle around creation in which all that happens is expressed. Thus the signs of the zodiac can be seen as gates to the *'Temple of Wisdom'*. They must all be experienced to gain experience and hopefully wisdom.

Virtue:

Devotion. This virtue is the only one that can be granted at this stage of spiritual development, as what else can be considered? Utter absorption of the divine.

Symbols:

The symbols of Chokmah are self-explanatory of its nature and are all masculine.

Binah:

'The third path is called the Sanctifying Intelligence, the foundation of Primordial Wisdom.
It is also called the creator of faith and its roots are in Amen.
It is the parent of faith, whence faith emanates.'

Titles:	Ama, the Dark Sterile Mother. Marah, the Great Sea. Aima, the Bright Fertile Mother.
Magical Imagery:	A Mature Woman.
God Name:	YHVH Elohim, meaning *'Lord Gods.'*
Archangel:	Tzaphkiel. The Watcher of God.
Angelic Orders:	The Aralim. The Thrones.
Mundane Chakra:	Saturn.
Spiritual Experience:	Vision of Sorrow.
Virtue:	Silence.
Vice:	Avarice.
Symbols:	The Vagina. Ark. Chalice. The Outer Robe of concealment. A Great and Stormy Sea.
Incense:	Civet or Myrrh.
Colour in Atziluth:	Crimson.
Colour in Briah:	Black.
Colour in Yetzirah:	Dark brown
Colour in Assiah:	Grey, flecked pink.

Binah, meaning understanding, is the third Sephira that has been created and is the totality of all femininity as can be seen from its symbology. Whereas Chokmah is assertive, Binah is receptive and is giving form to the force that is expressed via Chokmah; thus the play of force and form is brought into being. This formula holds many magical secrets and is the means of successful creation and the ensouling of talismanic designs at the lower levels of the everyday world.

Binah is the *'Ever Mother,'* she is the archetypal matron and whilst she can appear as both love and understanding she is also discipline and limitations. Force must be given the restriction of form or nothing will happen. This concept can be seen with the boiling kettle whereby the steam dissipates in the atmosphere, yet if it is contained appropriately it can drive the steam train, as Stephenson realised. Therefore without discipline all effort is wasted and nothing can be gained however promising the start may seem; for without Binah good ideas will come to naught.

Archangel:

Tzaphkiel is the archangel of Binah and the name means The Watcher of God. They can be considered as the archangel who oversees all that is created and is a concept of God being aware of creation.

Angelic Orders:

The Aralim are the angels of Binah and their title means thrones. Therefore Binah (understanding) becomes the throne of wisdom (Chokmah) and is the seat of divinity. They are responsible for the restrictions and disciplines of life.

Mundane Chakra:

This is the planet Saturn or Shabbatai, meaning the seventh as it is the seventh planet. The potencies of the planet Saturn can be seen as expressing the nature of Binah.

Virtue:

Silence is needed to hear the voice of the spirit, in other words the stopping of the endless chatter that goes through one's head all day every day. Through the discipline of meditation this endless distraction can be stilled whereupon a great calm silence steals over the mind bringing peace and balm to the soul. This emptying of the mind can take a lot of effort to achieve but is a useful occult discipline that needs regular working to gain its benefits.

Vice:

Avarice is the vice of Binah, something which we are all prone to, some more than others. Greed becomes a distraction from spirituality and can sometimes become a subtle challenge as well as a blatant vice. It is needs not wants that should be attended to as we go through life.

Symbols:

These are all self-explanatory and are all obviously feminine as they are symbols of receptivity.

Chesed:

The fourth path is called the Cohesive or Receptive Intelligence because it contains all the holy powers, and from it emanate all the spiritual virtues with the most exalted essences. They emanate one from another by virtue of the primordial emanation, the highest crown, Kether.

Titles:	Mercy. Gedulah. Love. Majesty. Benevolence.
Magical Imagery:	A Mighty Crowned and Enthroned King.
God Name:	El, meaning 'God.'
Archangel:	Tzadkiel. The Righteousness of God.
Angelic Orders:	Chasmalim. The Bright Shining Ones.
Mundane Chakra:	Jupiter.
Spiritual Experience:	The Vision of Divine Love.
Virtue:	Obedience.
Vice:	Bigotry, Gluttony, Hypocrisy and Tyranny.
Symbols:	The Crook or Sceptre. An Equal-Armed Cross.
Incense:	Cedar.
Colour in Atziluth:	Deep violet.
Colour in Briah:	Blue.
Colour in Yetzirah:	Deep purple.
Colour in Assiah:	Deep azure flecked yellow.

Chesed receives all the holy powers of creation from above and from there they flow throughout existence, hence the imagery of the king on his throne having dominion over all that is before him. Thus this Sephira is pouring out the force of creation and is seen as a potency of great abundance; this can be seen in the imagery and titles of Chesed: benevolence, majesty and mercy. The *Zohar* gives Chesed another title, Gedulah, which means majesty or greatness, which all express its attributes. El means God.

Archangel:

Tzadkiel is the archangel of Chesed and is heard as that inner voice that reminds us of the right thing to do. It is the archangel of doing the right thing, which is not always easy, as we find reasons not to do it!

Angelic Orders:

The Chasmalim are the angels of Chesed and are seen as the *'Bright Shining Ones'* who promote cheer, good will and well-being. They also grant comfort and hope to those who are distressed and who feel distraught.

Mundane Chakra:

This is the planet Jupiter, which is called Tzedek, who is seen in astrology as being the Great Beneficent.

Virtue:

Obedience to divine will and our fate, which is being enacted out during our lifetime, as an expression of the nature of God. Obedience to the divine plan and the role that we as spiritual individuals have to play within this can be seen as attributes of Chesed as we follow the natural flow of events in our lives and that of creation. We may feel that we are, or indeed should be, the centre of creation but we're not; but we are part of the cosmic drama that is being expressed and have an important role therein.

Vice:

The vices of Chesed are bigotry, gluttony and hypocrisy all of which can come about through the abuse of the generosity and plenitude of the nature of Chesed.

Symbols:

These are indicative of the majesty of Chesed and the beneficent nature of Jupiter.

Geburah:

'The fifth path is called the Radical Intelligence because it resembles unity, uniting itself to Binah, understanding, which emanates from the primordial depths of Chokmah, Wisdom.'

Titles:	Severity. Restriction. Justice. Strength.
Magical Imagery:	A Mighty Warrior King in his Chariot.
God Name:	Elohim Gibor, meaning *'Almighty God.'*
Archangel:	Khamael. The Burner of God.
Angelic Orders:	Seraphim. The Fiery Serpents.
Mundane Chakra:	Mars.
Spiritual Experience:	The Vision of Power.
Virtue:	Courage. Energy.
Vice:	Cruelty and Destruction.
Symbols:	The Sword. The Chain. A Sharp Point. A Five-Petalled Tudor Rose.
Incense:	Dragons Blood. Pepper
Colour in Atziluth:	Orange.
Colour in Briah:	Scarlet.
Colour in Yetzirah:	Scarlet.
Colour in Assiah:	Red, flecked black.

Geburah is the force of creation in action but it is also known as severity; such is its imagery of a mighty warrior king in action. Force can in excess become cruelty but we need force to get anything done as it is also our energy, effort and assertions. It is when it becomes unbalanced that it becomes a negative force of destruction, although destruction is also needed sometimes as it clears the ground to start again. This is also the Sephira of justice but not judgment. The God Name can be translated as *'Almighty God.'*

Archangel:

The archangel is Khamael who is seen as working with the forces of Chesed to keep equilibrium and is the protector of the weak and wronged when invoked to aid them.

Angelic Orders:

The Seraphim or Fiery Serpents are considered to clear out the unwanted and irrelevant aspects of life if they are approached for help in such matters.

Mundane Chakra:

This is the planet Mars also known as Madim and is seen by many in astrology as a malefic energy. This does not express its nature accurately, as this has been shown when considering the power of Geburah.

Virtue:

Courage and energy are important attributes that we need to face life, without them nothing can be done.

Vice:

Cruelty and destruction are the result of too much input from Geburah which is then imbalanced. However, little can be achieved that is of worth without the clearing out of the old to make way for the new.

Symbols:

The symbols such as the sword can be defensive as well as a symbol of aggression; such is the dual nature of Geburah. The Tudor Rose, with its five petals, is symbolic as the number five is the number of Geburah. The red and white can be interpreted in a sexual context.

Tiphereth:

'The sixth path is called the Mediating Intelligence because in it are multiplied the influxes of the emanations; for it causes that influence to flow into all the reservoirs of the blessings with which they themselves are united.'

Titles:	Beauty. Harmony. Sphere of the Sacred King. Melekh the King. The Lesser Countenance.
Magical Imagery:	A Child. Sacrificed God. Crowned King.
God Name:	YHVH Aloah Ve Daath, meaning *'Lord God made manifest in the sphere of the mind.'*
Archangel:	Mikael. The Perfect of God.
Angelic Orders:	Malachim. Kings.
Mundane Chakra:	Sun.
Spiritual Experience:	Vision of the Harmony of All Things. Mysteries of the Sacrifice of the Divine King.
Virtue:	Devotion to the Great Work.
Vice:	Pride.
Symbols:	The Rose Cross. Calvary Cross. Cube. The Lamen.
Incense:	Frankincense. Cinnamon. Abra-Melin.
Colour in Atziluth:	Rose pink.
Colour in Briah:	Yellow.
Colour in Yetzirah:	Salmon pink
Colour in Assiah:	Golden amber.

Tiphereth is the sixth Sephira and is the sphere of the sun. It has three God images that are used in meditations as these express its nature. The child is seen as the innocent spirit which is sacrificed (not literally!); the divine king who is resurrected as the crowned king. This imagery illustrates the stages to illumination, the *'Knowing of God.'*

The sun promotes growth and health, all aspects of Tiphereth, which promotes harmony. The God name translates as *'God made manifest in the sphere of the mind,'* which is a reference to the illumination that happens when contact between the higher and lower self takes place, *'The Great Work.'*

Thus all Solar Gods are Gods who bring healing and harmony; they're sacrificed but are also resurrected. The Christian story is but another account of this principle, which can be seen in the imagery of Tiphereth as meditative symbols towards enlightenment.

Archangel:

The archangel is Mikael, although some consider that the archangel of the sun is Raphael because of his healing attributes. Mikael is also associated with the element fire so is more fitting to be considered as the archangel of the sun.

Angelic Orders:

The Malachim or Kings are the kings of the four elements, the rulers of nature spirits and their mysteries.

Mundane Chakra:

The sun is sometimes known as Shemesh. The sun being seen as a healing and enlightening force that promotes growth and wellbeing. Without the sun no life on earth can exist: the Sun of God rather than the Son of God.

Virtue:

The virtue is one of *'Devotion to the Great Work.'* This is an alchemical term which is used to describe the one true goal of any real worth. A complete concentration, one-pointedness and surrender to the Union with God. The Great Work in alchemy is considered to be the transmutation of a base metal such as lead into the purity of gold in the literal sense as well as in a spiritual manner.

Vice:

Pride is associated with this Sephira, as it can be seen as being better then one's fellow man. This is why the Western Mysteries considered that it was important that one should *'desire to know in order to serve.'*

Symbols:

The Rose Cross is a symbol of the 15th century Rosicrucianism, and is one of inner harmony.

Netzach:

'The seventh path is called the Occult Intelligence because it is the refulgent splendour of the intellectual virtues which are perceived by the eyes of the intellect and the contemplations of faith.'

Titles:	Victory. Achievement.
Magical Imagery:	A beautiful naked woman.
God Name:	YHVH Tzabaoth, meaning *'God of Hosts.'*
Archangel:	Haniel. I, the God.
Angelic Orders:	Elohim. Gods.
Mundane Chakra:	Venus.
Spiritual Experience:	The Vision of Beauty Triumphant.
Virtue:	Unselfishness.
Vice:	Lust.
Symbols:	The Lamp, Girdle and Rose.
Incense:	Rose. Benzoin. Rosa Mystica. Red sandalwood.
Colour in Atziluth:	Amber.
Colour in Briah:	Emerald.
Colour in Yetzirah:	Yellowish-green.
Colour in Assiah:	Olive, flecked gold.

Netzach is the seventh Sephira and is titled Victory, the victory of achievement. It is also called the *'Occult Intelligence.'* Occult meaning hidden or in this case full of the mysteries. Feminine sexuality with its mysteries can be seen as an expression of this Sephira.

With its spiritual experience being of Beauty Triumphant, one can be reminded of another, little-acknowledged aspect of Lucifer, the Star of the Morning, who is wrongly associated with the Christian devil. The God Name is a reference to the hosts of nature which it rules.

Archangel:

The function of Haniel is to bring awareness of the Gods to mankind by an appreciation of the beauty of nature and the mystery thereof. This archangel also is influential over our emotions.

Angelic Orders:

These are the Elohim meaning Gods, that is the Gods of Nature. These angels represent the forces of nature and can be seen as the Gods of paganism.

Mundane Chakra:

This is the planet Venus which is known as Nogah. The Morning Star heralding the glory of the day and the forthcoming sunrise as glorious as an army with banners.

Virtue:

Unselfishness is the giving of the glories of Netzach, the sharing of the power of creation. *'Doing'* because it is right and meet to do so.

Vice:

Lust, which is deemed to be the vice, is perhaps the wanting of something which in itself isn't bad - after all how would humanity exist without it? But it can be detrimental when englamoured and one's thoughts dominated by it to the exclusion of everything else, and which subsequently leads to an adverse action.

Symbols:

The rose with its great beauty and scent can be seen as an apt symbol of Venus. It's also seen as the folds of the labia, so a feminine symbol. The girdle is the seven stars of *'The Great Bear'* with its own mysteries, seven being the number of Venus and Netzach. The Lamp is symbolic of the light of truth, Truth being a title of Netzach.

Hod:

'The eighth path is called the Absolute or Perfect Intelligence because it is the mean of the primordial which has no root by which it can cleave or rest save in the hidden places of Gedulah, from which it emanates its proper essence.'

Titles:	Glory. Splendour. Lesser Temple.
Magical Imagery:	A Hermaphrodite.
God Name:	Elohim Tzabaoth, meaning *'Gods of Hosts'*.
Archangel:	Raphael. The Healer of God.
Angelic Orders:	Beni Elohim. Sons of Gods.
Mundane Chakra:	Mercury.
Spiritual Experience:	The Vision of Splendour.
Virtue:	Truthfulness.
Vice:	Dishonesty.
Symbols:	The Holy Names. The Apron. The Cubic Stone.
Incense:	Lavender. Caraway. Fennel.
Colour in Atziluth:	Violet/Purple.
Colour in Briah:	Orange.
Colour in Yetzirah:	Russet red.
Colour in Assiah:	Yellowish-black, flecked white.

Hod is the eighth Sephira and means glory. It is the Sephira of the intellect and the mind. By its means forms are created on the subtle levels and are empowered, via the powers above, and driven down the planes to manifest their effects at the everyday levels. Man tends to anthropomorphise his Gods and the diverse aspects of God are active in the lower worlds. Thus mankind will create picture imagery of his Gods (form), which is an aspect of the powers of Hod, whilst they are ensouled by the forces of Netzach (force). Therefore all god forms belong to Hod and all god forces belong to Netzach.

The God name Elohim Tzabaoth translates as *'Gods of Hosts.'* These are the forms that clothe the forces of Netzach and thus make them more accessible to mankind via imagery. It is also associated with Hermes who has given his name to the Hermetic traditions of the occult; namely those involved with occult philosophies and the intellect, and the exploration of truth as well. This is the Sephira of the magical artes and the archetypal magician. With the concept of *'As above, So below'* that is, that which happens on the higher levels is reflected on the lower levels. An important occult truth.

Archangel:

The archangel is Raphael, the healer of God. Some systems will swap this archangel with Mikael of Tiphereth which adds some confusion to things. However Mikael is the archangel of fire so obviously solar. Raphael is the archangel associated with the element air and with the planet Mercury, therefore Hod is the more suitable association.

Angelic Orders:

The Beni Elohim or the Sons of Gods are the angels of Hod and are instrumental in mankind's construction of religious imagery as keys to access the subtle levels of creation.

Mundane Chakra:

This is the planet Mercury who stands the closest of all planets to the Sun and thus receives the most light. It is also known as Kokab.

Virtue:

Truth in all its aspects is the virtue of Hod. Truth can be experienced by knowledge which has been gained by those occult practices and philosophies which are of the nature of Hod.

Vice:

Falsity, dishonesty, these are the vices of Hod. Sometimes we deceive ourselves as well as others with knowledge which is abused or misunderstood.

Symbols:

The symbols of Hod, being the names, vesicles and apron, all relate to the fact that knowledge, which is contained in magical words and writings, is that by which the potencies of creation can be invoked. The apron is symbolic of the craftsman who performs the workings.

Yesod:

'The ninth path is called the Pure Intelligence because it purifies the emanations. It proves and corrects the designing of their representations, and disposes the unity with which they are designed without diminution or division.'

Titles:	Foundation. Treasure House of Images.
Magical Imagery:	A strong naked man.
God Name:	Shaddai El Chai, meaning *'Almighty Living God.'*
Archangel:	Gabriel. The Strong One of God.
Angelic Orders:	Kerubim. The Strong.
Mundane Chakra:	The Moon.
Spiritual Experience:	Vision of the Machinery of the Universe.
Virtue:	Independence.
Vice:	Idleness.
Symbols:	Perfumes. Sandals. The skrying mirror.
Incense:	White sandalwood. Aloes. Jasmine.
Colour in Atziluth:	Indigo.
Colour in Briah:	Violet.
Colour in Yetzirah:	Dark Purple
Colour in Assiah:	Citrine, flecked yellow.

Yesod is the ninth Sephira and is the etheric plane, that level of existence that is just beyond our everyday world. It is where matter is shaped and formed by the forms and forces from above; this is the level where magic is created. It is the world that holds up the material world which is symbolised by the image of the strong man, yet because of its receptivity it is also seen as being feminine. Magical philosophy would claim that it is at this level that disease and illness first manifests, and it is also where we feel pain. Therefore Yesod holds the image of everything that exists in the material world which explains the reference to the *'Treasure House of Images.'*

Archangel:

The archangel of Yesod is Gabriel who is also associated with the element water and the moon. Both of these are of a reflective nature which equates with the quality of Yesod. However as all the forces of the Sephira above are expressed through Yesod into Malkuth the everyday world, Gabriel is seen as the announcer, a fact which can be seen in Christianity with the announcement to Mary of her forthcoming pregnancy. Yesod rules over pregnancy and birth, which can be seen as the gateway into the world.

Angelic Orders:

The Kerubim are the angels of Yesod who harness the etheric forces behind our everyday world. It is here that the subconscious mind resides and is the gateway to the worlds beyond.

Mundane Chakra:

The Moon is the celestial body that is associated with Yesod, she is also known as Levanah. All lunar Goddesses are aspects of the forces of Yesod. The Moon rules all tides of growth and the ebb and flow of events that happen in the world. This is affected by the lunar phases that revolve from the new to the full moon and through to the last quarter. The virgin, mother and crone.

Virtue:

Independence of the everyday world is what is indicated here, whereby one is not dictated to by the demands of the everyday and that one has the body under control with its incessant demands. Then without distraction an exploration of the Holy Tree can take place.

Vice:

Knowing what it is that one should do and not doing it is idleness, and with idleness one is not independent and there can be no going forward.

Symbols:

Scent can be very suggestive and this is the realm of aromatherapy and the power of incense.

Malkuth:

> *'The tenth path is called the Resplendent Intelligence because it is exalted above every head and sits upon the throne of Binah. It illuminates the splendours of all the lights and causes an influence to emanate from the Prince of Countenances, the Angel of Kether.'*

Titles:	The Kingdom. The Inferior Mother. Kallah the Bride. Gate of Tears. Gate of Death.
Magical Images:	A young woman crowned and throned.
God Name:	Adonai Ha-Aretz, meaning *'Lord of the Earth'*.
Archangel:	Sandalphon. Brotherly One.
Angelic Orders:	Ashim. The souls of fire.
Mundane Chakra:	The sphere of the elements.
Spiritual Experience:	Vision of the Holy Guardian Angel.
Virtue:	Discrimination.
Vice:	Inertia.
Symbols:	The equal-armed cross. Altar of the double cube. The magical circle and the triangle of manifestation.
Incense:	Storax. Patchouli.
Colour in Atziluth:	Yellow.
Colour in Briah:	Citrine, olive, russet and black.
Colour in Yetzirah:	As above but flecked with gold.
Colour in Assiah:	Black, rayed with yellow.

Malkuth is the tenth Sephira and is where the energies of the Tree are made manifest and is the everyday world that we all inhabit. The physical world holds the key to self-awareness and a raising of consciousness and expanding of awareness. Man incarnates into the physical world as a spirit enclothed within a physical body. He is equipped with a full range of senses and is also armed with a wide range of emotions and an intellectual capacity of varying ability. This gives him the means to experience life at this level and to act accordingly. He is like the deep sea diver who is encased in a heavy diving suit to experience life at the bottom of the ocean. He receives his oxygen through a tube from above or he would die. Such is man who has incarnated here in the physical world, whereby he is the spirit wearing the fleshy body and is attached to the heavenly realms from whence he draws the sustenance that is needed to maintain him. At death the body breaks down and returns to the earth which has fed and provided for it; for this is the natural cycle of events. The spirit is released as it can then return to the subtle levels from whence it came.

'Should the golden bowl be broken and the silver cord loosen.'
(Ecclesiastes 12:6)

This is a biblical reference to the life force that is deemed to be seen around a person's head and the cord that connects the spirit to the physical body during the lifetime of the individual. We graze in the fields of earth and we lie down in the fields of heaven to chew the cud. We need to be able to grasp life at this level and cope with it, far too long has the occult world been the haven of the mentally unstable and dysfunctional who in many cases simply entrench their own inadequacies. Yet the occult is the supreme science that grants the knowledge of mankind and his relationship with God and is worthy of a lifetime study and practice. The lesson of Malkuth is to cope with it, life cannot be run away from, only those people who have their feet firmly on the ground can reach into the heights of heaven.

Archangel:

The archangel is Sandalphon who is the guide and the intelligence of earth; the world of the everyday.

Angelic Orders:

The Ashim are the angelic orders of Malkuth, they are often depicted as fiery beings armed with swords who guard the entrance to the holy Tree, much in the manner of mankind's expulsion from the Garden of Eden. To regain entry to the higher levels man must balance those aspects of his being which are chaotic and negative. Then with some inner harmony attained he is in a far better position to approach the Tree of Life.

Mundane Chakra:

This is the sphere of the four elements and the four cardinal points. The elements of fire, water, air and earth relate to the divine letters Yod – Heh – Vav – Heh, the Tetragrammaton, the four-lettered name of God. They are also represented by the astrological symbols of Leo, Scorpio, Aquarius and Taurus. These are the fixed signs of the zodiac and are thus at their most dense.

The elementals of fire are the salamanders, of water the undines, of air the sylphs and of earth the gnomes. Each order has its role in maintaining the well-being of life on earth and all that which is manifest here.

The king of air and the realm of the sylphs is Paralda. Of fire and the realm of the salamanders is Djinn. Of water and the realm of the undines is Niksa. Of earth and the realm of the gnomes is Ghob.

These are the four elemental kings who oversee the workings of their respective elements. They can be seen as spiritual illuminated elementals, placed by God to oversee the workings of the world.

> *'Therefore be prompt and active as the sylphs And not boastful nor squanderous.*
> *Be brave and courageous as the salamanders But not cruel.*
> *Be loving and giving as the undines Yet not selfish.*
> *Be thou patient and steadfast as the gnomes And not greedy.*
> *So shalt thee master the powers of the soul.'*
>
> (from the Mass of On-nophris - Ordo Dei)

Virtue:

Discrimination is the virtue needed to make choices to go forward or stay as one is.

Vice:

Inertia is the vice of being unaware of one's spirituality or doing nothing with it. Inert clay born.

Symbol:

The symbols of the magical circle and triangle relate to practical magic. This is the defining of a given area within which to work, with the triangle being where the entities from the other worlds are summoned to manifestation by the magician and is therefore a symbol of containment and restriction.

CHAPTER FOUR

'The Paths of the Tree'

There are twenty-two paths on the Tree which all relate to a Hebrew letter, various symbols, tarot cards, planets and astrological signs. Through various techniques of meditation they can be explored and experienced. The methods can be as simple or complex as one's sense of the arte demands. Whilst a Sephira can be seen as an objective state, the experience of the paths that link each Sephira is subjective. Thus each individual will have a different experience, although there will be aspects that are experienced in common.

The symbols of the path are seen as being threefold. Primarily there is the symbol of the Hebrew letter which will be associated with the path. They follow a particular pattern with Aleph the first letter being associated with the first path from Kether to Chokmah, then following a strict alphabetical order until the last path is reached between Yesod and Malkuth where the last letter Tau will be associated.

The second attribution is the astrological signs, classical planets and the elements air, fire, water and earth. These will all be attributed to a Hebrew letter and are keys to accessing the paths of the Tree. Thirdly there is the association of the Tarot Trumps which are assigned to each path and can be used in themselves as doorways to these levels.

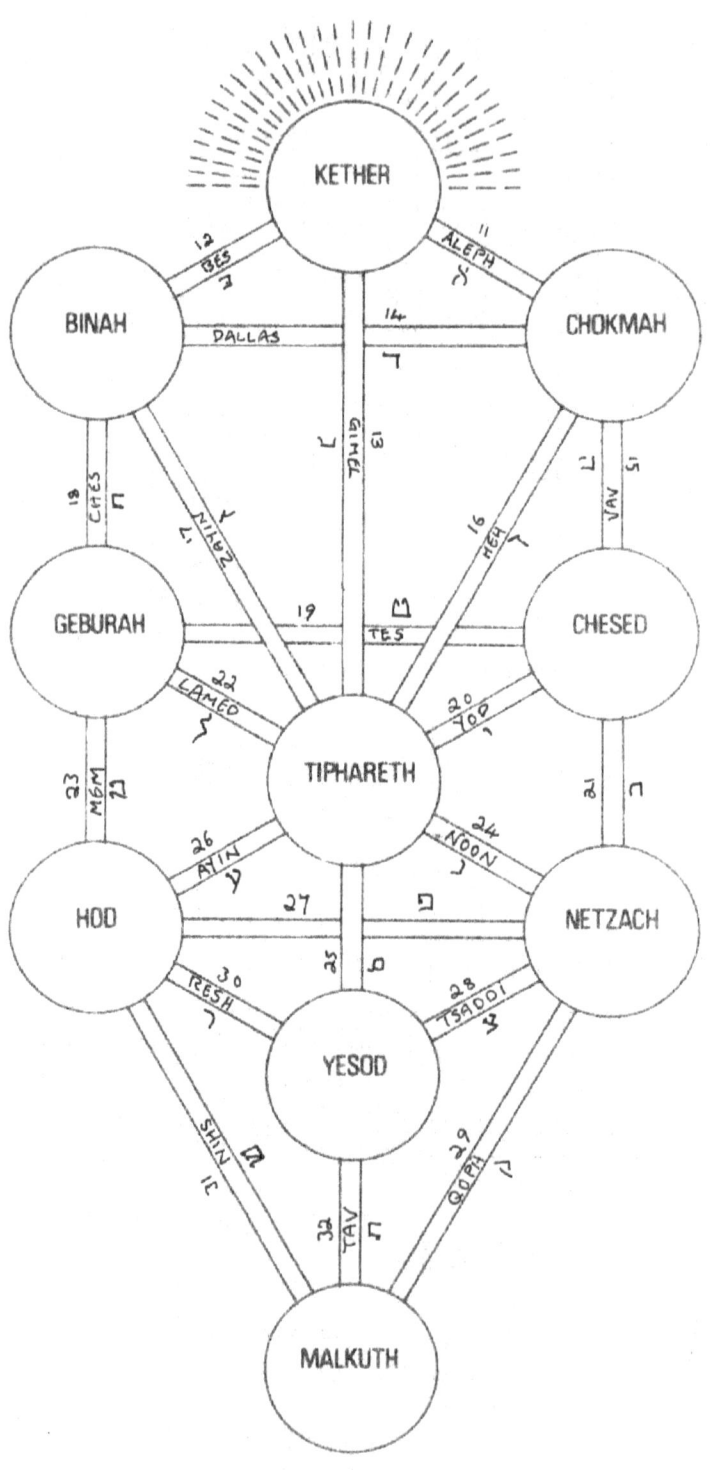

11th Path: Aleph

'The eleventh path is called the Scintillating Intelligence because it is the essence of that curtain which is placed close to the order of the disposition and this is a special dignity given to it that it may be able to stand before the face of the Cause of Causes.'

Divine Name of the Path	Ehieh
Linking	Kether – Chokmah
Letter	Aleph, meaning Ox
God Names	Eheieh – YHVH
Archangelic	Metatron – Ratziel
Angel	Aiah
Element	Air
Images	Swastika. Eagle
Incense	Galbanum
Tarot Card	The Fool
Magical Weapons	Wand – Pentacle
Colour in Atziluth	Yellow
Colour in Briah	Sky blue
Colour in Yetzirah	Blue, emerald green
Colour in Assiah	Emerald, flecked green

Seal of Angel Aiah:

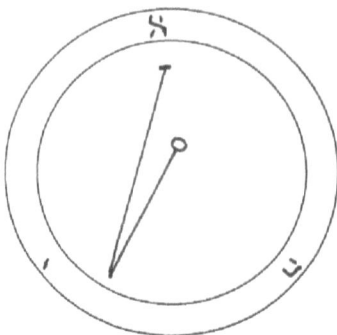

This is the first path, the out rush of divine breath, hence its association with the element air. Air is also associated with spirit, is unconfined, and permeates all things in existence. Air is also the great disperser.

This path is represented by the Fool who is seen as the wise fool, an archetype that is found globally. Whilst his lack of experience may seem to be a disadvantage it is an advantage in some respects as his mind is uncluttered and open to new experiences. Like air he cannot be contained, for as the madman on the edge of society he goes his own way ignoring the concepts with which society binds the individual. He is the herald of new life.

This is the path of important decisions and choices, also of unexpected influences. Its negative aspects are self undoing and reckless behaviour.

Invocation of Aleph: Elohim Eheieh - God of Gods

'Blessed are the undefiled in the way, who walk in the law of the Lord.
Blessed are those who keep his testimonies and seek him with the whole heart
They also do no iniquity, they walk in his ways.
Thou has commanded us to keep thy precepts diligently.
O that my ways were directed to keep thy statues then shall I not be ashamed,
when I have respect unto all thy commandments.
I will praise thee with uprightness of heart when I shall have learned thy righteous judgments.
I will keep thy statutes, O forsake me not utterly.'

12th Path: Beth

'The twelfth path is the Intelligence of Transparency because it is the species of magnificence called Chazchazit, the place whence issues the vision of those seeing in apparitions.'

Divine Name of Path:	Bachour
Linking	Kether – Binah
Letter	Beth, meaning House
God Names	Eheieh – YHVH Elohim
Archangelic	Metatron – Tzaphkiel
Angel	Biah
Planet	Mercury
Images	The Ibis. The Magician at his altar
Incense	Mastic
Tarot Card	The Magician
Magical Weapons	Sword, Chalice, Wand and Pentacle
Colour in Atziluth	Yellow
Colour in Briah	Purple
Colour in Yetzirah	Grey
Colour in Assiah	Indigo, flecked violet

Seal of the angel Biah

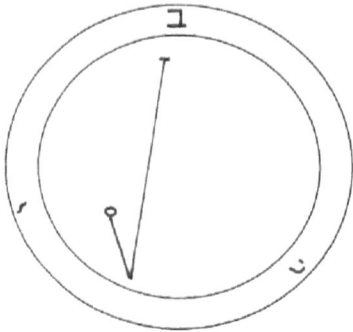

This path represents the highest ideal of magical awareness of God and will reveal the nature of the divine. The granting of spiritual knowledge is the function of this path and is seen in the Yetziratic texts with the reference to *Chazchazit* meaning seership or spiritual knowledge at its highest. This path grants a perception of spiritual truths and what really is and one's relationship to it.

The tarot trump The Magician is associated with this path; he is seen as being a forceful character who is self-confident and stands alone. He is the adept who has all aspects of his being in equilibrium and by the power of his will manifests power in the material worlds. By the power of his will he is in control of the four elements with the symbol above his head being symbolic of his divinity which is in accordance with divine will.

This is the path of self-confidence and will-power. Its negative aspect is failure of nerve and hesitation.

Invocation of Beth: Elohim Bachur – Chosen God

> 'Wherewithal shall a young man cleanse his way? By taking heed thereto according to thy word.
> With my whole heart have I sought thee O let me not wander from thy commandants.
> Thy word I have hid in my heart, that I might not sin against thee.
> Blessed art thou O Lord teach me thy statues.
> With my lips I have declared all the judgments of thy mouth.
> I have rejoiced in the ways of thy testimonies as much as in all riches.
> I will meditate in thy precepts and I have respect unto thy ways.
> I will delight myself in thy statues I will not forget thy word.'

ג

13th Path: Gimel

'The thirteenth path is named the Uniting Intelligence and is so called because it is itself the essence of glory. It is the consummation of truth of individual spiritual things.'

Divine Name of Path:	Gadol
Linking	Kether – Tiphereth
Letter	Gimel, meaning Camel
God Names	Eheih – YHVH Eloah Ve Daath
Archangel	Metatron – Mikael
Angel	Giah
Planet	Moon
Images	A bow and arrow, A dog howling at full moon
Incense	Camphor
Tarot Card	The Priestess
Magical Weapon	Wand, Chalice
Colour in Atziluth	Blue
Colour in Briah	Silver
Colour in Yetzirah	Pale blue
Colour in Assiah	Silver rayed blue

Seal of the angel Giah

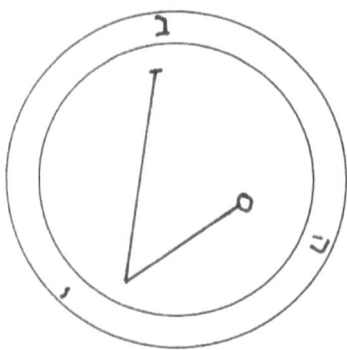

The vertical paths 13th, 25th and 32nd are straight up the Tree to Kether, and are the paths of the mystic, referred to as *'The Path of the Arrow.'* These paths are solely concerned with the Union with God and often the student will experience what is termed the *'Dark Night of the Soul,'* an experience full of doubt and questioning which must be gone through as much of the dross of the soul is encountered and must be dealt with so that the *'Wine of the Spirit'* may be poured into a stable vessel.

This is the path of the abyss, a state that exists between Kether and Tiphereth where much of the murk of the soul dwells. Here are all those traits that we are in denial of, but which are part of our own psyche. Here can be found *'The Shadow, the Dweller on the Threshold.'* The manifestation and personification of our faults will be experienced on this path. These must be assimilated and transmuted into the gold of the spirit. The symbolism of the camel crossing the dessert under a night sky is often seen as depicting this path and its experience.

Real and true initiation is an experience of realisation which can come about through prolonged spiritual striving; this is a natural process of spiritual growth which will take time to manifest. Initiation ceremonies should mirror this process, thus the coming out of darkness into the light. You cannot buy initiation, it is granted from upon high.

This is also the path of the High Priestess tarot card, also known as the Priestess of the Silver Star. She is the great feminine force that controls the source of all life. Thus she is seen as sitting between two pillars, one positive the other negative. She is the passive link that is between the physical and the spiritual realms, through her it is said that God is made manifest in the heart of man. Her title is *'The Indwelling*

Glory.' She is the Shekinah who brings inspiration to the soul of man and is the source of all intuitive knowledge. Through her the divine can be made manifest upon earth. The veil behind her is the thin curtain between the conscious mind and the deeps of the subconscious.

The positive attributes of this path are the revealing of that which is hidden or obscured. The granting of intuitive insight. The negative aspects are those of emotional instability and problems arising from ignoring sound advice.

Invocation of Gimel: Elohim Gadol – Great God

'*Deal bountifully with thy servant that I may live and keep thy word.*
Open thou mine eyes that I may behold wondrous things of thy law.
I am a stranger in the earth hide not thy commandments from me.
My soul breaketh for the longing that it hath unto thy judgment at all times.
Thou has rebuked the proud that are cursed which do err from thy commandments. Remove from me reproach and contempt, for I have kept thy testimonies.
Princes did also sit and speak against me, but thy servant did mediate in thy statutes.
Thy testimonies are also my delight and my counsellors.'

ד

14th Path: Daleth

'The fourteenth path is the Illuminating Intelligence and it is so-called because it is that Chasmal which is the founder of the concealed and fundamental ideas of holiness and of the stages of preparation.'

Divine Name of Path	Dagoul
Linking	Chokmah – Binah
Letter	Daleth, meaning Door
God Name	YHVH – YHVH Elohim
Archangel	Ratziel – Tzaphkiel
Angel	Diah
Planet	Venus
Images	A door. The girdle, a dove and the lamp
Incense	Sandalwood and Myrtle
Magical Weapons	The Wand, Chalice and Lamp.
Tarot Card	The Empress.
Colour in Atziluth	Emerald green.
Colour in Briah	Sky blue.
Colour in Yetzirah	Spring green.
Colour in Assiah	Bright rose, rayed pale green.

Seal of the angel Diah

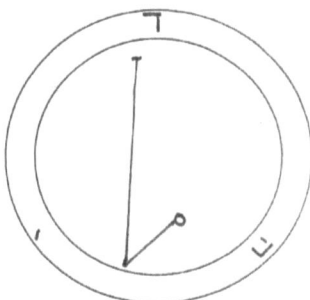

The position of this path between the archetypal concepts of masculine and feminine polarity, which are attributed to Chokmah and Binah, is a path of illumination. It is also known as the Daughter of the Mighty Ones as she is depicted as sitting on a throne in a wheat field and is an aspect of the feminine side of God which is denied by Christianity.

The tarot card the Empress is the obvious imagery for this path and is associated with Venus and all her attributes. For she embodies the potency of nature together with the feminine wisdom of the Queen of Life. She is concerned with life being expressed on the physical levels. Her pregnant figure reveals her as the guardian of motherhood. The power of the empress is passive and is expressed through the emotions and feelings. This path can grant a spiritual awakening through the contemplation and appreciation of the powers of nature. The key is to discern the workings of heaven in the kingdom of nature and thus the realisation that material worlds are but the garment of the divine by which we can perceive the workings of God.

This path grants fertility in all its aspects, she gives abundance, maternal care and protection. The negative aspects can be seen as domestic upheavals, poverty and sterility.

Invocation of Daleth: Elohim Dagul – Well-Known God

'My soul cleaveth unto the dust quicken thou me according to thy word
I have declared my ways, and thou hearest me teach me thy statutes.
Make me to understand the way of thy precepts so shall I talk of

thy wondrous works.
My soul melteth for heaviness strengthen thou me according to thy word.
Remove from me the way of lying and grant me thy law graciously.
I have chosen the way of truth thy judgments have I laid before me, I have stuck unto thy testimonies
O Lord put me not to shame. I will run the way of thy commandments when thou shalt enlarge my heart.'

15th Path: Heh

The fifteenth path is the Constituting Intelligence, so called because it constitutes the substance of creation in pure darkness and men have spoken of the contemplations; it is the darkness spoken of in scripture, Job XXXIII:9 'And thick darkness a swaddling band for it'.'

Divine Name of Path	Hadom
Linking	Chokmah – Tiphereth
Letter	Heh, meaning Window
God Name	YHVH - YHVH Eloah Ve Daath
Archangel	Ratziel – Mikael
Angel	Hiah
Zodiac	Aries
Images	A Ram. Water and Wine
Incense	Dragons Blood gum
Magical Weapons	Sword and Chalice
Tarot Card	Emperor
Colour in Atziluth	Scarlet
Colour in Briah	Red
Colour in Yetzirah	Orange/red
Colour in Assiah	Red

Seal of the angel Hiah:

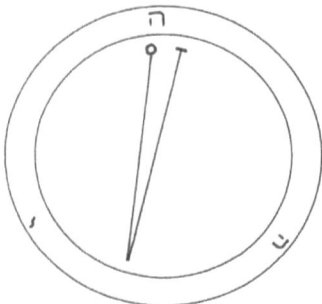

Aries is the astrological sign that is attributed to this path and it is the first of the astrological signs. As the sign is associated with Mars the colours are as one would expect, those of fire. This is the sign of spring and the beginning of new life after the dark of winter.

The tarot card the Emperor shows a man who is God consecrated and holds the land and all that dwells therein to be in his care, a sacred trust that can only be bestowed from upon high.

This is the path that grants the spiritual freedom that can occur when the adversities of life have been engaged and assimilated through struggle and experience. This will give an increase in will-power and self-control, it also grants the knowledge that is acquired through experience. Its adverse nature is one of immaturity, weakness, failure and loss of influence.

Invocation of Heh: Elohim Adu – Magnificent God

> 'Teach me O Lord the way of thy statutes and I shall keep it unto the end.
> Give me understanding and I shall keep thy law Yea I shall observe it with my whole heart.
> Make me to go in the path of thy commandments for therein do I delight.
> Incline my heart unto thy testimonies
> and not to covetousness. Turn away mine eyes from beholding vanity and quicken thou me in thy way.
> Establish thy word unto thy servant Who is devoted to thy fear?
> Turn away my reproach which I fear, For thy judgments are good.
> Behold I have longed after thy precepts Quicken me in thy righteousness.'

ו

16th Path: Vau

'The sixteenth path is the Triumphal or Eternal Intelligence because it is the pleasure of the glory beyond which there is no other glory like to it and it is also called the paradise prepared for the righteousness.'

Divine Name of Path	Vezio
Linking	Chokmah – Chesed
Letter	Vau, meaning Nail
God Name	YHVH – El
Archangel	Ratziel – Tzadkiel
Angel	Viah
Zodiac	Taurus
Image	A Bull
Incense	Storax
Magical Weapons	Wand and Pentacle
Tarot Card	The Pope
Colour in Atziluth	Red-orange
Colour in Briah	Indigo
Colour in Yetzirah	Olive
Colour in Assiah	Brown

Seal of the angel Viah

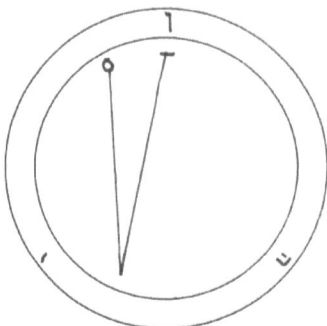

The tarot card The Pope is associated with this path and implies spiritual wisdom and insight into the mind of God. He is the representative of God on earth; therefore we can see this path bearing within it the energies that manifest at the lower levels. Jungian concepts would say that this is the path of the informing spirit which initiates the individual into the meaning of life and explains its secrets according to the teachings of old. The teacher of traditional wisdom who reveals that which is hidden.

This path will grant information to life's problems; however on a negative level it will mis-inform and give bad advice.

Vau: Elohim Vesio – Splendorous God

> 'Let thy mercies come also unto me O Lord even thy salvation according to thy word.
> So shall I have wherewith to answer him that reproacheth me for I trust in thy word.
> And take not the word of truth utterly out of my mouth for I have hoped in thy judgments.
> So shall I keep thy law continually forever and ever. And I will walk at liberty for I seek thy precepts.
> I will speak of thy testimonies also before kings and will not be ashamed.
> And I will delight myself in thy commandments which I have loved. My hands also will I lift up unto thy commandments, which I have loved and I will meditate in thy statutes.'

17th Path: Zain

'The seventeenth path is the Disposing Intelligence which provides faith to the righteous and they are clothed with the Holy Spirit by it, and it is called the foundation of excellence in the state of higher things.'

Divine Name of Path	Zakai
Linking	Binah – Tiphereth
Letter	Zain, meaning Sword
God Name	YHVH Elohim – YHVH Eloah Ve Daath
Archangel	Tzaphkiel – Mikael
Angel	Ziah
Zodiac	Gemini
Image	A Magpie
Incense	Wormwood
Magical Weapons	Sword, Wand and Chalice
Tarot Card	The Lovers
Colour in Atziluth	Orange
Colour in Briah	Light mauve
Colour in Yetzirah	Pale yellow
Colour in Assiah	Reddish-grey

Seal of the angel Ziah

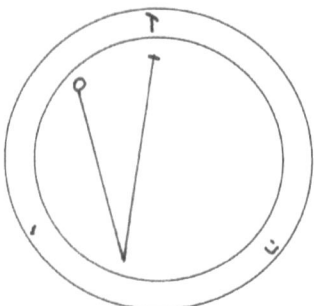

This is the path that grants the spirit the knowledge of its incarnatory destiny, the meaning of its life and its purpose. The sign of Gemini, who are twins, shows the true relationship between the higher and lower self. The lower self will ultimately become a mirror image of the higher self and thus they will reflect one another.

The potency of this path will help to develop intuition as inspiration from the higher self manifests. Whilst the negative aspects are those of indecision and hesitancy.

Invocation of Zain: Elohim Zakai – Pure God

> 'Remember the word unto thy servant upon which thou has caused me to hope
> This is my comfort in my affliction, for thy word hath quickened me.
> The proud hath had me greatly in derision yet have I not declined from thy law?
> I remembered thy judgments of old, O Lord and have comforted myself.
> Horror hath taken hold upon me because of the wicked that forsake thy law.
> Thy statutes hath been my songs in the house of my pilgrimage.
> I have remembered thy name O Lord in the night and have kept thy law.
> This I had because I kept thy precepts.'

18th Path: Cheth

'The eighteenth path is called the Intelligence of the House of Influence (by the greatness of whose abundance the influence of good things upon created beings is increased), and from its midst the arcana and hidden senses are drawn forth which dwell in its shade and which cling to it from the cause of all causes.'

Divine Name of Path	Hasid
Linking	Binah - Geburah
Letter	Cheth, meaning Fence
God Name	YHVH Elohim – Elohim Gibor
Archangel	Tzaphkiel - Khamael
Angel	Chiah
Zodiac	Cancer
Images	Sphinx, Chariot
Incense	Lotus
Magical Weapons	Sword and Chalice
Tarot Card	The Chariot
Colour in Atziluth	Amber
Colour in Briah	Maroon
Colour in Yetzirah	Russet
Colour in Assiah	Greenish-brown

Seal of the angel Chiah:

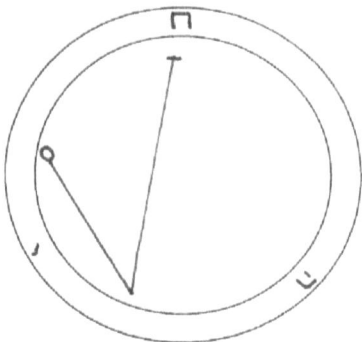

The eighteenth path is referred to as the House of Influence as this path is a channel between the spirit and the personality and is thus spiritual activity in action. This path will grant success, despite the obstacles that life produces. It is the path of victory over adversity, victory that is attained by the power of the will rather than good luck or inheritance. However its negative side is one of egocentricity and ruthlessness; the ignoring of the rights of others.

Invocation of Cheth: Elohim Chesed - Merciful God

Thou art my portion, O Lord I have said that I would keep thy word.
I entreated thy favour with my whole heart be merciful unto me according unto thy word.
I thought on my ways and turned my feet unto thy testimonies.
I made haste and delayed not to keep thy commandments.
The bands of the wicked have robbed me but I have not forgotten thy law.
At midnight I will rise to give thanks unto thee because of thy righteous judgments.
I am a companion of all them that fear thee and of them that keep thy precepts.
The earth O Lord is full of thy mercy teach me thy statutes'

19th Path: Teth

'The 19th path is the Intelligence of the Secret of all the activities of spiritual beings and is so called because of the influence diffused by it from the most high and sublime glory.'

Divine Name of Path	Tehod
Linking	Geburah - Chesed
Letter	Teth, meaning serpent
God Name	Elohim Gibor - El
Archangel	Khamael - Tzadkiel
Angel	Tiah
Zodiac	Leo
Images	Sword. Wand
Incense	Frankincense
Tarot Card	Strength
Colour in Atziluth	Green-yellow
Colour in Briah	Deep purple
Colour in Yetzirah	Grey
Colour in Assiah	Red – yellow

Seal of the angel Tiah

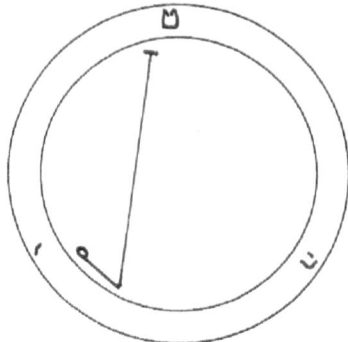

This path is concerned with karma and divine justice, and is one of the main paths of the Tree as it falls on the Lightning Flash, that is the paths that are traversed as the force travels down from Kether from Sephira to Sephira until it reaches Malkuth. Working with the energies of this path can cause conflicts within the individual which must be worked out before progress can take place. As Jung has said, *'The Self is made manifest in the opposites and in the conflict between them.'* It is a *'coincidentia oppositorum.'* Thus the route to the Self begins with conflict. This path can grant the opportunity to put one's plans into action, if one has the courage to see them through. The negative force is one of defeat which comes about through a failure of nerve.

Invocation of Teth: Elohim Theor – Spotless God

'Thou hast dealt well with thy servant, O Lord according to thy word.
Teach me good judgment and knowledge for I have believed thy commandments. Before I was afflicted I went astray but now I have kept my word.
Thou art good and doest good teach me thy statutes The proud have forged a lie against me,
but I will keep thy precepts with my whole heart.
Their heart is as fat as grease but I delight in thy law.
It is good for me that I have been afflicted that I might learn thy statutes.
The law of thy mouth is better unto me than thousands of gold and silver.'

י

20th Path: Yod

'The twentieth path is the Intelligence of Will and is so called because it is the means of preparation of all and each created being, and by this intelligence the existence of the primordial wisdom becomes known.'

Divine Name of Path	Iah
Letter	Yod, meaning hand
Linking	Chesed - Tiphereth
God Name	El – YHVH Aloah Ve Daath
Archangel	Tzadkiel - Mikael
Angel	Iiah
Zodiac	Virgo
Image	Hermit
Incense	All virginal odours
Magical Weapons	Wand and Lamp
Tarot card	The Hermit
Colour in Atziluth	Yellowish-green
Colour in Briah	Grey
Colour in Yetzirah	Green-grey
Colour in Assiah	Plum

Seal of the angel Iiah:

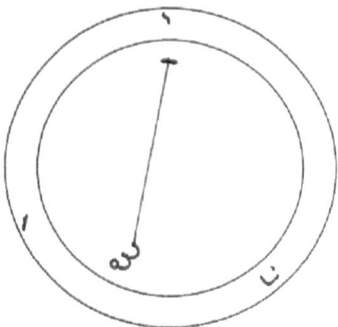

The twentieth path grants insights into destiny; this is the path of the individual who is seeking meaning to their existence. The purpose of voluntary isolation is to increase psychic awareness of one's condition and immediate environment, thus the role of the hermit will promote the conditions that are needed for psychic development to unfold. To abandon conventional values in favour of the inner promptings of the soul is to set the individual apart from society. This is a solitary path that not all have the strength of personality to endure. The Hermit can be the *'Wise Old Man'* who appears as a symbol sometimes in dreams, particularly in moments of sustained emotional crisis. This is the path that promotes good advice with life's problems and will offer solutions or bring about opportunities to resolves situations, if one can grasp them.

Invocation of Yod: Elohim Yah – Divine God

'Thy hands have made me and fashioned me give me understanding that I may learn thy commandments.
They that fear thee will be glad when they see me Because I have hoped in thy word.
I know O Lord that thy judgments are right and that thou in faithfulness hast afflicted me.
Let I pray thee, thy merciful kindness be for my comfort according to thy word unto thy servant.
Let thy tender mercies come unto me that I may live for thy law is my delight.
Let the proud be ashamed for they dealt perversely with me without a cause
but I will meditate in thy precepts.'

21st Path: Kaph

The twenty-first path is the Intelligence of Conciliation and Reward it is so called because it receives the divine influence which flows into it from its benediction upon all and each existence.'

Divine Name of Path	Kabir
Letter	Kaph, meaning palm of hand
Linking	Chesed - Netzach
God Name	El- YHVH Tzabaoth
Archangel	Tzadkiel - Haniel
Angel	Kiah
Zodiac	Jupiter
Images	Wheel. Chalice
Incense	Rose and cedar
Magical Weapons	Pentacle and Lamp
Tarot card	Wheel of Fortune
Colour in Atziluth	Violet
Colour in Briah	Blue
Colour in Yetzirah	Purple
Colour in Assiah	Blue-rayed yellow

Seal of the angel Kiah

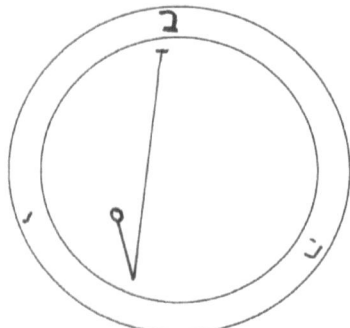

This path grants knowledge of the *'Will of the Spirit'* through the emotions. This can create the yearning for pastures new and the sense that there must be a bigger picture which one is part of. This path inspires the seeker.

The tarot card of The Wheel can be seen as a Mandala in a Jungian sense, the wheel being an image of psychic wholeness and inner order. This path will assist in granting new influences of a beneficial nature to enter one's life, and is the path of good luck. It grants opportunities that promote one's well-being and good fortune.

Invocation of Kaph: Elohim Kabir – Powerful God

'My soul fainteth for thy salvation
But I hope in thy word, My eyes fail for thy word saying, when wilt thou comfort me?
For I am become like a bottle in the smoke, yet do I not forget thy statutes.
How many are the days of thy servant? When wilt thou execute judgment on them that persecute me?
The proud have digged pits for me which are not after thy law.
All thy commandments are faithful they persecute me wrongfully, help thou me.
They had almost consumed me upon earth but I forsook not thy precepts.
Quicken me after thy loving kindness so I shall keep the testimony of thy mouth.'

22nd Path: Lamed

'The twenty-second path is the Faithful Intelligence and is so called because by it spiritual virtues are increased and all dwellers on earth are nearly under its shadow.'

Divine Name of Path	Limmud
Linking	Geburah - Tiphereth
Letter	Lamed, meaning Ox Goad
God Name	Elohim Gibor – YHVH Aloah Ve Daath
Archangel	Khamael
Angel	Liah
Zodiac	Libra
Image	Lightning Flash
Incense	Galbanum
Magical Weapons	Sword and Spear
Tarot card	Justice
Colour in Atziluth	Emerald
Colour in Briah	Blue
Colour in Yetzirah	Blue-green
Colour in Assiah	Light green

Seal of the angel Liah:

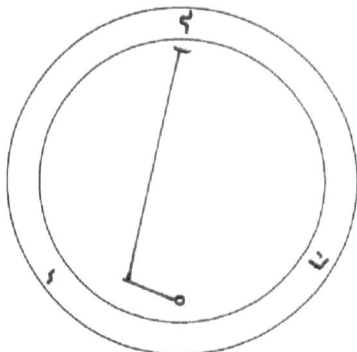

This is a path that is often considered to be one of restoring internal balance and will bring the individual to face those aspects which they are ignoring. This is done to promote inner harmony and balance. Sometimes this will also manifest on the outer levels in the individual's everyday life. The image of the letter Lamed being an ox goad suggests that this path will drive the spirit on and that it cannot deviate from its course as it evolves, there is no rest until attainment is reached. This path can also be seen as the inner voice that urges the spirit on as it makes it aware that the needs of the conscious mind and body, having been served, have done nothing to assimilate the forces of the subconscious, which must have a means of expression or an imbalance will occur which will disrupt the well-being of the psyche. This is the path of judgment and justice at all levels and in all situations.

Invocation of Lamed: Elohim Limud – Knowing God

> 'For ever O Lord thy word is settled in Heaven Thy faithfulness is unto all generations thou hast established the earth and it abideth.
> They continue this day according to thine ordinances for all are thy servants.
> Unless thy law had been my delights I should then have perished in mine affliction.
> I will never forget thy precepts
> The wicked have waited for me to destroy me But I will consider thy testimonies.
> I have seen an end of all perfection but thy commandment is exceeding broad.'

23rd Path: Mem

'The twenty-third path is the Stable Intelligence and is so called because it has the virtue of consistency among all numerations.'

Divine Name of Path	Meborak
Linking	Geburah - Hod
Letter	Mem, meaning water
God Name	Elohim Gibor – Elohim Tzabaoth
Archangel	Khamael - Raphael
Angel	Miah
Zodiac	Water
Images	Chalice and Wand
Incense	Myrrh
Magical Weapon	Mirror
Tarot card	Hanged Man
Colour in Atziluth	Deep blue
Colour in Briah	Sea green
Colour in Yetzirah	Olive green
Colour in Assiah	White flecked purple

Seal of the angel Miah:

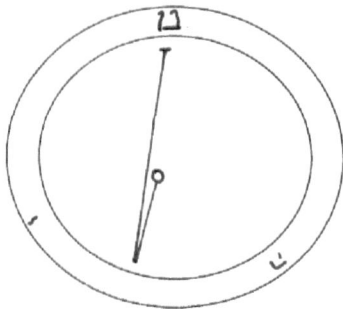

This is a path of reflection, something that may be considered of the nature of water which is associated with this path and thus psychism. It is also associated with the subconscious levels of the mind wherein are contained all manner of forces which must be assimilated. When the conscious mind plumbs the depths of its own psyche the consciousness can be seen to put itself in peril, but it is only by exploring and coming to terms with the dark and unknown side of man can the individual make any worthwhile progress.

'Man Know Thy Self' as the Greek Mysteries declared. This is something which this path will do as it throws up challenges and observations regarding the human condition. This is the path that will help the seeker to align themselves with divine will rather than the laws and social restrictions of society. This is the path of the individual mind therefore the herd mentality will not pass this path.

Invocation of Mem: Elohim Maborak – Praiseworthy God

> 'O how I love thy law, It is my meditation all the day thou through thy commandments hast made me wiser than mine enemies for they are ever with me.
> I have more understanding than all my teachers for thy testimonies are my meditation.
> I understand more than the ancients because I keep thy precepts.
> I have refrained my feet from every evil way that I might keep thy word.
> I have not departed from thy judgments for thou has taught me.
> How sweet are thy words unto my taste Yea, sweeter than honey to my mouth.
> Through thy precepts I get understanding therefore I hate every false way.'

24th Path: Nun

ן

'The twenty-fourth path is the Imaginative Intelligence and is so called because it gives a likeness to all the similitudes which are created in like manner to its harmonious elegancies.'

Divine Name of Path	Nora
Linking	Tiphereth - Netzach
Letter	Nun, meaning Fish
God Name	YHVH Aloah Ve Daath – YHVH Tzabaoth
Archangel	Mikael - Haniel
Angel	Niah
Zodiac	Scorpio
Images	Scorpion. Fish. Ram
Incense	Opoponax
Magical Weapons	Dagger and Chalice
Tarot card	Death
Colour in Atziluth	Green-blue
Colour in Briah	Brown
Colour in Yetzirah	Dark brown
Colour in Assiah	Indigo brown

Seal of the angel Niah:

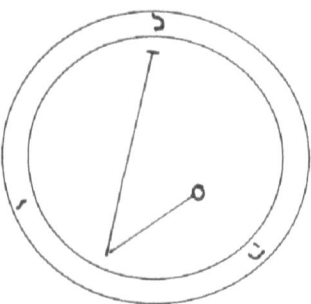

This path has much to do with change that is part of the natural cycle of events but nonetheless can be uncomfortable and unwelcome. It is the logical process of evolution. Sex and death, both which are associated with the sign Scorpio, are the means by which humans come and go from this world and can therefore be seen as gateways that grant ingress to worlds beyond the everyday. This path is on the lightning flash therefore its energies will promote a more vigorous experience in the life of the student who is working with this path as the energies are assimilated by the soul. When rising up the Tree from Malkuth, this path can promote a crisis as the individual approaches Tiphereth, which must be faced, and its lessons absorbed. This path can bring about major change which is necessary for the individual, such as the removing of that which is outgrown so that the soul can move forward, not always easy or painless.

Invocation of Nun: Elohim Norah – Formidable God

> 'Thy word is a lamp under my feet
> and a light unto my path I have sworn and I will perform it that I will keep thy righteous judgments.
> I am afflicted very much: quicken me O Lord according unto thy word
> Accept, I beseech thee, the freewill offerings of my mouth, O Lord and teach me thy judgments.
> My soul is continually in my hand yet do I not forget thy law.
> The wicked have laid a snare for me, yet I erred not from thy precepts.
> Thy testimonies have I taken as a heritage forever. For thou are the rejoicing of my heart.
> I have inclined my heart to perform thy statutes always even unto the end.'

25th Path: Samekh

'The twenty-fifth path is the Intelligence of Probation or Temptation and is so called because it is the primary temptation, by which the Creator trieth all righteous persons.'

Divine Name of Path	Somek
Linking	Tiphereth - Yesod
Letter	Samekh, meaning Prop
God Name	YHVH Aloah Ve Daath – Shaddai El Chai
Archangel	Mikael - Gabriel
Angel	Siah
Zodiac	Sagittarius
Image	Arrow
Incenses	Cassia and Myrrh
Magical Weapons	Spear and Chalice
Tarot card	Temperance
Colour in Atziluth	Blue
Colour in Briah	Yellow
Colour in Yetzirah	Green
Colour in Assiah	Dark blue

Seal of the angel Siah:

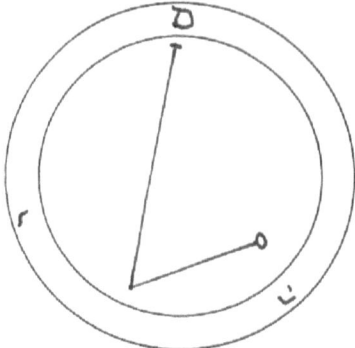

This is the path that can lead to the first real experiences of the Higher Self, residing at Tiphereth. This can be a testing time which will cause the individual to question everything that they do. In severe cases this will be the *'Dark Night of the Soul,'* and can be a deeply troubling spiritual experience whilst it lasts. It is an initiation in its own right into the higher worlds. Faith will be the only prop which will avail the soul as it journeys onwards, all the energies of the will and body must be one-pointed, like the arrow, as one's aim is firmly fixed on the experience of Tiphereth. Then and only then will the sun rise for the aspirant, as the dark lifts, and the power of the Sun manifests in the life of the individual.

The image of the tarot card Temperance is the soul which has a foot in both the worlds of the conscious and subconscious worlds.

This is the path of success only if all the factors that are involved are carefully managed to get the best out of the situation. However mishandling of the energies of this path will hamper the individual in their spiritual journey.

Invocation of Samekh: Elohim Somek – Supporting God

'I hate vain thoughts but thy law do I love.
Thou art my hiding place and my shield I hope in thy word.
Depart from me ye evil doers: for I will keep thy commandments of my God. Uphold me according to thy word that I may live and let me not be ashamed of my hope.
Hold thou me up and I shall be safe and I will have respect unto thy statutes continually.
Thou hast trodden down all them that err from thy statutes for

there deceit is falsehood.
Thou puttest away all the wicked of the earth like dross therefore I love thy testimonies.
My flesh trembleth for fear of thee and I am afraid of thy judgments.'

26th Path: Ayin

'The twenty-sixth path is called the Renewing Intelligence because the Holy God renews by it all the changing things which are renewed by the creation of the world.'

Divine Name of Path	Hazaz
Linking	Tiphereth - Hod
Letter	Ayin, meaning Eye
God Name	YHVH Aloah Ve Daath – Elohim Tzabaoth
Archangel	Mikael - Raphael
Angel	Aiah
Zodiac	Capricorn
Images	Goat, Lingam and Yoni
Incense	Musk
Magical Weapons	Wand and Chalice
Tarot card	Devil
Colour in Atziluth	Indigo
Colour in Briah	Black
Colour in Yetzirah	Blue-black
Colour in Assiah	Dark grey

Seal of the angel Aiah:

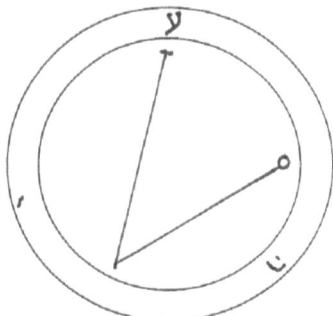

This path represents the illusion of the intellectual views that unless they are balanced by Tiphereth consciousness will become an illusion of God. This imagery can become full of the bigotry of priestcraft and the repressed negativity of the group or individual soul, thus creating false imagery of God and mankind's role in creation. This path will grant access to the mysteries of Tiphereth, but first the individual must come to terms with that which opposes him. These are the forces of negativity that are deep within his subconscious, both on a personal level and also on a far greater collective level that belongs to humanity. This can be seen as the Christian devil, the shadow side of mankind's collective activity. The devil, which the priests of Christianity have used for centuries to 'chapel whip' their flock into a narrow fold. This is the path that will help the seeker to assimilate the contents of their subconscious mind and make known that which is unknown.

Invocation of Ayin: Elohim Hazaz – Strong God

> 'I have done judgment and justice leave me not to my oppressors
> Be surety for thy servant for good, Let not the proud oppress me.
> Mine eyes fail for thy salvation and for the word of thy righteousness.
> Deal with thy servant according unto thy mercy and teach me thy statutes.
> I am thy servant give me understanding that I may know thy testimonies.
> It is time for thee Lord to work for they have made void thy law.
> Therefore I love thy commandments above gold yea above fine gold.
> Therefore I esteem all thy precepts concerning all things to be right and I hate every false way.'

27th Path: Peh

'The twenty-seventh path is called the Active or Existing Intelligence and it is so called because through it every existent being receives its spirit and motion.'

Divine Name of Path	Phodeh
Linking	Netzach - Hod
Letter	Peh, meaning Mouth
God Name	YHVH Tzabaoth – Elohim Tzabaoth
Archangel	Haniel - Raphael
Angel	Piah
Zodiac	Mars
Images	Wolf, Horse
Incense	Pepper
Magical Weapons	Chalice, Pentacle and Sword
Tarot card	Tower
Colour in Atziluth	Scarlet
Colour in Briah	Red
Colour in Yetzirah	Red
Colour in Assiah	Red, rayed azure and green

Seal of the angel Piah:

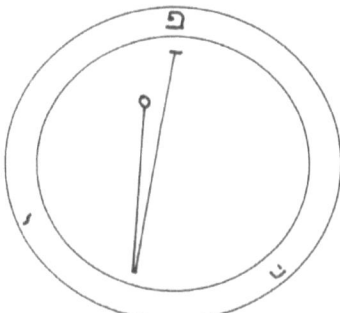

This is the main path of the soul which links the powers of feeling – Netzach, with thought – Hod. These are the primary means by which mankind can experience life at this level: thought and feeling. The tarot card The Tower shows how devastating the energies of this path can be if unprepared, and even then the unexpected can bring all down. The individual must have their feet firmly on the ground if they think that they can reach for the heights of heaven otherwise they will fail in their endeavour.

This path can bring down false imagery of one's self and it will promote questioning of one's values and goals. Sometimes situations will arise which will seem to be acts of fate which will bring this about. These can be seen as part of the initiation into the mysteries of this path and are often an uncomfortable experience.

Invocation of Peh: Elohim Phodeh – Redeeming God

> 'Thy testimonies are wonderful therefore doth my soul keep them.
> The entrance of thy words giveth light it giveth understanding unto the simple.
> I open my mouth and I panted for I longed for thy commandments.
> Look thou upon me and be merciful unto me as thou doeth unto those who love thy name.
> Order my steps in thy word and let not any iniquity have dominion over me.
> Deliver me from the oppression of man so I will keep thy precepts.
> Make thy face to shine upon thy servant and teach me thy statutes.
> Rivers of waters run down my eyes, Because they keep not thy law.'

28th Path: Tzaddi

'The twenty-eighth path is called the Natural Intelligence; by it is completed and perfected the nature of all that exists beneath the sun.'

Divine Name of Path	Tzedek
Linking	Netzach - Yesod
Letter	Tzaddi, meaning Fish Hook
God Name	YHVH Tzabaoth – Shaddai El Chai
Archangel	Haniel - Gabriel
Angel	Tziah
Zodiac	Aquarius
Images	Eagle, Olive Tree
Incense	Galbanum
Magical Weapons	Chalice and Dagger
Tarot card	The Star
Colour in Atziluth	Violet
Colour in Briah	Sky-blue
Colour in Yetzirah	Blue-mauve
Colour in Assiah	White, tinged purple

Seal of the angel Tziah:

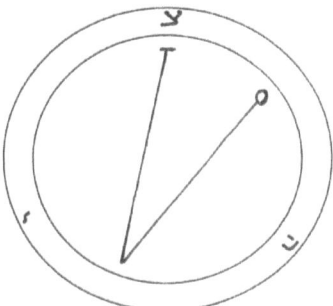

This is the path that allows the creative forces of Netzach to pour into the subconscious mind at Yesod, and is the path of creative inspiration. It is a path that is easily contacted and can exert a strong power of glamour on the individual who is a weak character. The forces of Netzach are intimately associated with Lucifer who is not the Christian devil but the great light-bearing angel who awakens mankind to their spiritual nature. This is the path of faery and the worlds of elfhame. This is the mystery of the Holy Graal, the making of one's self ready and purified to invoke and to hold the higher forces of spirituality. For as the mysteries of Mithras declare, *'I am a star that wanders with you and shines from the depths.'* This is the path that gives insights into possibilities, it gives new life and power to cope with adversity.

Invocation of Tzaddi: Elohim Tzedek – Just God

'Righteous art thou O Lord and upright are thy judgments
Thy testimonies that thou hast commanded are righteous and very faithful.
My zeal hath consumed me because mine enemies have forgotten thy words.
Thy word is very pure therefore thy servant loveth it.
I am small and despised yet I do not forget thy precepts.
Thy righteousness is an everlasting righteousness and thy law is the truth.
Trouble and anguish have taken hold of me yet thy commandments are my delights.
The righteousness of thy testimonies is everlasting give me understanding and I shall live.'

29th Path: Qoph

'The twenty-ninth path is the Corporeal Intelligence so called because it forms every body which is formed in all the worlds and the reproduction of them.'

Divine Name of Path	Kadosh
Linking	Netzach - Malkuth
Letter	Qoph, meaning Back of Head
God Name	YHVH Tzabaoth – Shaddai El Chai
Archangel	Haniel - Sandalphon
Angel	Quiah
Zodiac	Pisces
Image	Fish
Incense	All sweet odours
Magical Weapons	Dagger, Pentacle and Chalice
Tarot card	The Moon
Colour in Aziluth	Crimson
Colour in Briah	Buff, flecked silver white
Colour in Yetzirah	Pink-brown
Colour in Assiah	Stone-coloured

Seal of the angel Quiah:

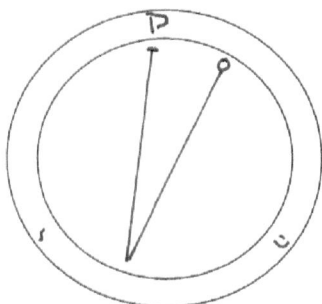

This path is concerned with the survival of the species, hence its concerns with the animal drives of mankind and the sexual reproduction thereof. It is expressed through mankind's basic instincts and a reminder that nature is both red in tooth and claw. This is the path of accepting the reality of human nature and the Way of Nature, sometimes referred to as the Green Way. This is the path that is associated with Lilith, the woman who was before Eve, of whom it is said in *Isaiah* XXXIV, that, *'the satyr shall cry to his fellow, the screech owl shall also rest there and find for herself a place of rest. There shall the Great Owl make her nest.'* Thus the imagery of Lilith being banished to the wild places is but an aspect of the sexuality of the Beautiful Naked Woman of Netzach.

The tarot card imagery shows the desolation and the fear to go forward. This is the path that shows that the individual only has themselves to rely upon.

Invocation of Qoph: Elohim Kadosh – Holy God

> *'I cried with my whole heart hear me O Lord I will keep thy statutes.*
> *I cried unto thee save me and I shall keep thy testimonies I prevented the dawning*
> *of the morning and cried I hoped in thy word.*
> *Mine eyes prevent the night watches that I might meditate in thy word.*
> *Hear my voice according unto thy loving kindness O Lord quicken me according to thy judgment.*
> *They draw nigh that follow after mischief they are from the law.*
> *Thou art near O Lord and all thy commandments are truth.*
> *Concerning thy testimonies I have known of old that thou hast founded them forever.'*

ר

30th Path: Resh

'The thirtieth path is the Collective Intelligence and astrologers deduce from it the judgment to the stars and celestial signs and perfect their science according to the rules of the motion of the stars.'

Divine Name of Path	Rodeh
Linking	Hod - Yesod
Letter	Resh, meaning Sun
God Name	Elohim Tzabaoth – Shaddai El Chai
Archangel	Raphael - Gabriel
Angel	Riah
Zodiac	Sun
Images	Lion, Sunflower
Incenses	Cinnamon or frankincense
Magical Weapons	Chalice, Pentacle and Wand
Tarot card	The Sun
Colour in Atziluth	Orange
Colour in Briah	Golden yellow
Colour in Yetzirah	Rich amber
Colour in Assiah	Amber, rayed red

Seal of the angel Riah:

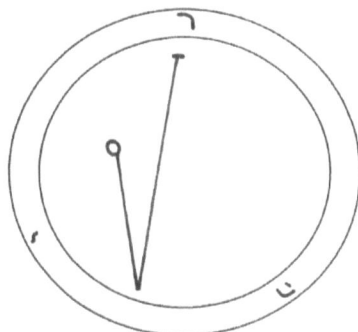

This is the path of the inner spiritual sun which is symbolised by the sun high in the noon-time sky. The path will convey thoughts into the subconscious mind, there to digest and manifest in time, as can be seen with hypnosis. This is also the path of intellectual illumination and enlightenment, the path of the Hermetic Ray, the path of the attainment of wisdom. The power of the intellect and emotion are both combined at Yesod, the subconscious. This can be seen as two children who are united and playing in a garden, which is depicted in some tarot cards; the card of psychic wholeness and well-being of the soul. This path grants success against great odds, and gives safety against the perils of life.

Invocation of Resh: Aloha Rode – Commanding God

'Consider mine affliction and deliver me for I do not forget thy law. Plead my cause and deliver me quicken me according to thy word Salvation is far from the wicked for they seek not thy statutes.
Great are thy tender mercies
O Lord quicken me according to thy judgments. Many are my persecutors and mine enemies Yet do I not decline from thy testimonies.
I beheld the transgressors and was grieved because they keep not thy word.
Consider how I love thy precepts quicken me O Lord according to thy loving kindness.
Thy word is true from the beginning and every one of thy righteous judgments endureth forever.'

31st path: Shin

'The thirty-first path is the Perpetual Intelligence but why is it so called? Because it regulates the motions of the sun and moon in their proper order, each in an orbit convenient for it.'

Divine Name of Path	Shaddai
Linking	Hod – Malkuth
Letter	Shin, meaning tooth
God Name	Elohim Tzabaoth – Adonai Ha Aretz
Archangel	Raphael – Sandalphon
Angel	Shiah
Element	Fire
Image	Lion
Incenses	Frankincense and copal
Magical Weapons	Wand, Lamp and Pentacle
Tarot card	Judgment
Colour in Atziluth	Orange-scarlet
Colour in Briah	Vermillion
Colour in Yetzirah	Scarlet flecked gold
Colour in Assiah	Vermillion, flecked crimson and gold

Seal of the angel Shiah

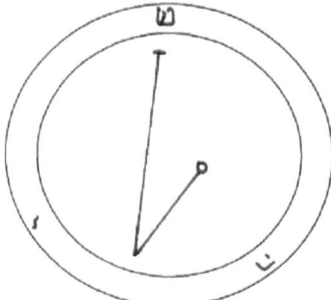

The thirty-first path is the path that will help to understand the personality of the individual and will reveal the mental factors involved within the mind. The path will help to promote the living-out of spiritual principles rather than mental theorizing. It is also the path of the home fire and the fire that allows mankind to survive the hostility of the natural world without which it is unlikely that mankind could have evolved or survived. This is the family principle in action and it also will reveal karmic actions that are playing out in one's life.

This is the path of good health and the return thereto. It is also the path that grants new starts in life and gives pleasure in achievements.

Invocation of Shin : Elohim Shaddai – Almighty God

> 'Princes have persecuted me without a cause, but my hand standeth in awe of thy word.
> I rejoice at thy word as one that findeth great spoil I hate and abhor lying but thy law do I love
> Seven times a day do I praise thee because of thy righteous judgments.
> Great peace have they which love thy law and nothing shall offend them.
> Lord I have hoped for thy salvation and done thy commandments.
> My soul have kept thy testimonies and I love them exceedingly.
> I have kept thy precepts and thy testimonies, for all my ways are before thee.'

ת

32nd Path: Tau

'The thirty-second path is the Administrative Intelligence and it is so called because it directs and associates the motions of the seven planets directing all of them in their proper courses.'

Divine Name of Path	Thechinah
Linking	Yesod - Malkuth
Letter	Tau
God Name	Shaddai El Chai – Adonai Ha Aretz
Archangel	Gabriel - Sandalphon
Angel	Thiah
Zodiac	Saturn
Images	Ash Tree, Sickle
Incenses	Storax, all heavy perfumes
Magical Weapons	Pentacle, Chalice
Tarot card	The World
Colour in Atziluth	Indigo
Colour in Briah	Black
Colour in Yetzirah	Blue-black
Colour in Assiah	Black rayed blue

Seal of the angel Thiah:

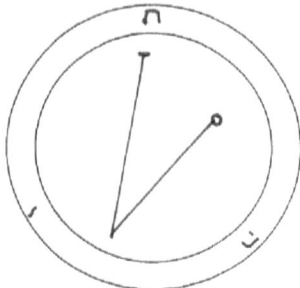

The thirty-second path joins the physical world with the levels of the universal unconscious, where all of mankind's experiences are held. This is the path of the first steps of spiritual evolution, whereby spirit shall experience and understand the implications of manifestation and the nature of God.

This is also the path of birth and death; it is amply illustrated by the tarot card The World. The tarot card imagery is clear that the search is neither beginning or ending, as death is but a birth into the next levels of existence, as physical birth is a death for the spirit to the inner planes from whence it has come and unto which it will return.

This path will either begin a new round of experience or help to close one that is finished, the ending of a cycle of destiny.

Invocation of Tau: Elohim Teguinah – Favourable God

> 'Let my cry come before thee O Lord give me understanding according to thy word.
> Let my supplication come before thee deliver me according to thy word.
> My lips shall utter praise when thou has taught me thy statutes.
> My tongue shall speak of thy word for thy commandments are righteous.
> Let thine hand help me for I have chosen thy precepts.
> I have longed for thy salvation O Lord and thy law is my delight.
> Let my soul live and it shall praise thee and let thy judgments help me.
> I have gone astray like a lost sheep seek thy servant for I do not forget thy commandments.'

CHAPTER FIVE

Praxis - The Work

'My power is in the name of the Lord who hath made heaven and earth!
O Lord, hear my prayer and let my cry come unto thee'

(The Rite of the Summons.... Ordo Dei)

It is true that little can be achieved in any sphere of life unless effort is placed therein, and it is the same with any aspect of the magical path. To gain access to this mystery one has to develop one's powers of concentration, visualization and will, for without these little of substance will be gained. Regular daily exercises that require the use of these powers are required and the following exercises and practices will go some considerable way to developing these attributes.

The daily use of such practices as the Lesser Banishing Ritual of the Pentagram (LBRP), so beloved by Western Occultists, and the use of the Middle Pillar working will not only help to develop these attributes but will also aid in promoting emotional, mental and psychic well-being at all levels. By regular use of these two magical practices other magical modes of operation will suggest themselves to the operator as both workings can be expanded into other forms of ritual such as evocation, talismans and general workings, which will be found to be of interest and use..

The use of colour, drama and incense are also to be found to be useful when creating suitable magical ritual; something that the church has forgotten to its detriment.

Lesser Banishing Ritual of the Pentagram:

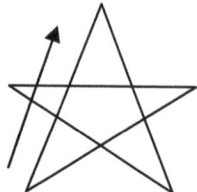

The pentagram ritual was created by MacGregor Mathers and the Golden Dawn one hundred and twenty years ago based, I believe, upon the suggestions that are to be found in Eliphas Levi's work *Transcendental Magic*. This was published in France during the mid-nineteenth century and was a popular commentary on Levi's conception of magic which went on to influence a generation of magical students.

The working starts by facing east and by the performance of the Kabbalistic Cross. The wording is in Hebrew and is a reference to various Sephiroth on the Tree of Life. The English translations indicate that whoever formed the Lord's Prayer was conversant with Kabbalistic concepts.

Facing east raise your right hand above your head and visualise a bright sphere above you. Intone firmly, and this can be done silently, the wording *'Ateh.'* Which means, *'Thou art.'* Bring your hand down to the heart region and touch your chest as you visualise the light travelling downwards through your body to your feet, and here intone, *'Malkuth.' 'The kingdom.'* Touching your right shoulder intone *'Ve - Geburah.' 'And the power.'* Whilst bringing your hand across to your left shoulder visualise the light travelling from right to left, thus forming a cross within you. As you touch the left shoulder intone, *'Ve – Gedulah.' 'And the glory.'* Clasp your hands in front of your chest and declare, *'Le –Olam Amen.' 'Forever Amen.'*

Amen, the ending to so many Christian prayers means, *'Lord Faithful King,'* and is a word that is created from the Hebrew letters Aleph, Mem and Nun. Within the Kabbalah is the practice of Notariqon, a way of creating new words from the first letters of sacred words and is a form of magical shorthand. Another practice is to swap numbers for the letters; by adding them up one can compare them to the numbers of other letters to try and access their hidden relationships, as it is deemed that letters and words with the same number will have some relationship if their hidden meaning can be accessed. Both David

Rankine and Israel Regardie have illustrated this practice in their works on the Kabbalah.

After the Kabbalistic Cross come the inscriptions of the pentagrams. The pentagram can be seen as the image of mankind dominant over the four elements. The top being spirit with the left arm water, right arm air, bottom right fire and bottom left earth. There are astrological reasons as to why this is laid out as such, which are taken from the positions of the zodiac. When the pentgram is laid on the zodiac the fixed signs of Leo = fire, Taurus = earth, Scorpio = water and Aquarius = air will be found to be at the end of each of the pentagram's arms. Spirit at the top being man, thus representing the perfected man in harmony with his inner being.

The first pentagram is traced in the east after the K/C starting at the bottom left corner as this is a banishing rite. This will be the same pentagram at each of the quarters and is to be visualised in a glowing white colour. The pentagrams will need to be about three feet or so high. The first one, when created, is activated by stabbing the centre and intoning the word, 'YHVH' - Yod – Heh – Vav – Heh. Visualise the pentagram moving away from you out into the eastern quarter and as it does so it clears the area of anything that is negative to the working. Now with your arm out stretched trace a line from the right arm of this pentagram to the southern quarter and repeat the tracing of the pentagram and when charging the pentagram intone, 'Adonai.' Again visualise the pentagram push away from the southern quarter anything averse to the working that is to be performed. Bring the light from the pentagram to the western quarter and repeat the visualisation and intone the wording, 'Eh – Heh – Yeh.' Finally bring the line around to the northern quarter and again repeat, using the name 'AGLA.' And close in the east by forming your circle.

With this operation you should have now traced a complete circle around you with a charged pentagram at each of the four compass points. Standing in the centre of your circle stretch your arms out to form a cross and visualise a tall yellow robed figure in the east, beyond the edge of your circle, and intone, 'Before me, Raphael.' Visualising a blue robed figure behind you, intone 'Behind me Gabriel.' Now see on your right hand a tall figure robed in red and declare, 'On my right hand, 'Mikael.'

See on your left a tall figure robed in the dark colours of the earth and intone, 'On my left, Auriel.' See the circle with the four pentagrams at the compass points with the figures standing behind them and say,

'About me flame the pentagrams.' Visualise a six-pointed star on your back whilst saying, *'Behind me shines the six-rayed star.'* Finish with the Kabbalistic Cross. This is basically the LBRP which can be expanded into other workings of a more complex nature.

Middle Pillar:

This is a useful Kabbalistic working that is based on the Tree of Life and can be adapted for a wide range of magical workings should you so choose to do so, with daily use of this practice being beneficial. Its basic practice is to visualise from the top of the head to the feet a shaft of light that runs through the body. At various points along its length are visualised five spheres of different coloured light that correspond to the middle pillar on the Kabbalistic Tree of Life. These spheres are visualised intently, whilst their God Name is intoned.

This can be done silently or audibly as one wishes. By visualising these spheres and also by building up within them various symbols that are relevant to them or placing one's consciousness therein, if even momentarily, you will greatly enliven them.

This practice can in time can be developed to include visualization of the whole of the Tree within one's auric field, with its connecting paths, which again will add much to the working. There are several methods of circulating the energies around the aura, which, if accompanied by intent, will enhance the work. It can furthermore be developed to be used in various magical workings which I explore in the work *Liber Noctis*.

Otz Chim

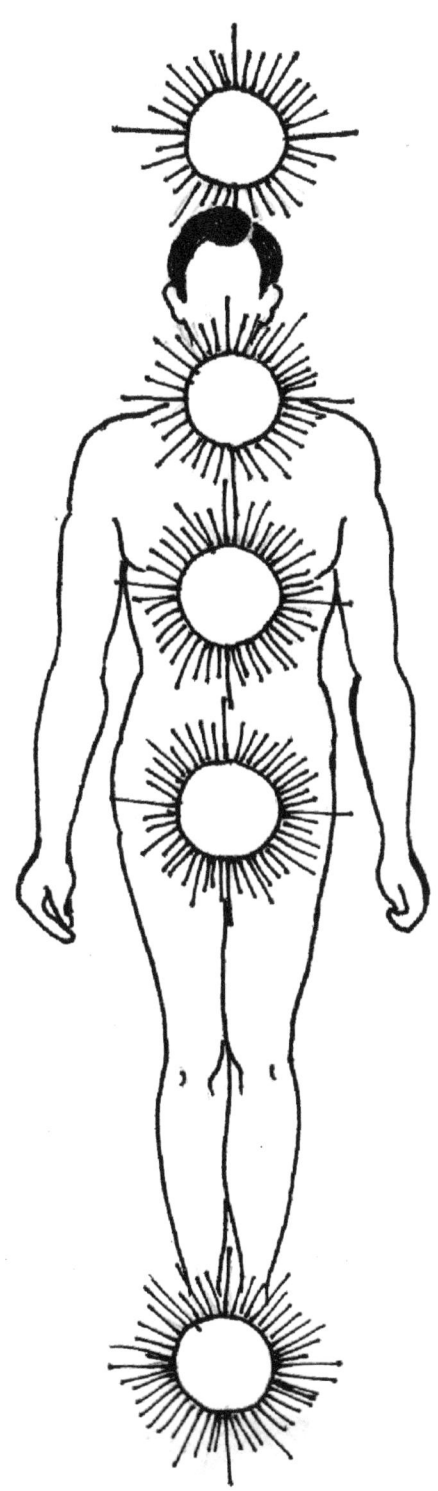

The Middle Pillar Exercise

Face east and concentrate on the area above your head, this can be done either standing or sitting, and build the image of a sphere of brilliant light and place within it your consciousness and intone the God Name Eh – Yeh – Heh.

The sphere will sometimes feel as if it is tingling at this point and you will become much more aware of it as a presence. Let the light then travel downwards to the area at your throat and build up a lavender-coloured sphere, again place your consciousness within and intone YHVH Elohim.

Bring the light from this sphere down to the heart region and build up the imagery of a glowing pink sphere, the colour of sunrise. Place your consciousness therein and intone the God Name YHVH Aloah Ve Daath.

Bring the light next downward to the region of one's genitalia and visualise a sphere of indigo light forming, again placing one's consciousness therein intone the God Name Shaddai El Chai.

Finally bring the light down to your feet and let the sphere form that is coloured yellow. As before place one's consciousness within and intone Adonai Ha Aretz.

With the establishing of this the Middle Pillar we can now circulate the energy by visualising the top sphere. As one breathes out let the light travel down the left side of the body to the feet and enter the bottom sphere. As you breathe in it travels up the right-hand side of the body back to the top sphere. Perform this three times and then visualise the light traveling down the front of the body to the bottom sphere as you breathe out and as you breathe in let it travel up the back of your body to the top sphere. Again perform this visualisation three times. See the auric field around you glow brilliantly.

This simple working will make a useful daily magical exercise and will be found to be beneficial. As you visualise the auric field around you state with intent that you are well or perhaps happy or indeed anything that you feel is necessary to your well-being.

A second approach is to visualise the crown at the top of your head and then see the energy flow out and over you as the spray of a fountain. This is done on an out-breath. Then see the energies being drawn into the Malkuth sphere at your feet and as you breathe in let them flow up the Middle Pillar and be reabsorbed at the crown. This exercise can be done several times. It can also be done after the circulation of the light around the body as previously shown or after the working.

This can be accompanied by prayers and invocations; incense can be useful as an aid. By combining this with the LBRP which would need to be performed first one can create a suitable daily rite which will greatly enhance one's well-being and develop your powers of concentration and visualisation. It can also in itself become an initiation into the mysteries of the Tree of Life.

If you are keen on developing your healing skills after performing the Middle Pillar working you can quite easily pour the energies via your hands into a sick person, animal or object to work as you will. This may have to be done several times as it will depend on the amount of energies that you are able to summon, but repetition will enforce the working. By visualising the auric field being flooded with the relevant colours and intoning the appropriate God Name, planetary workings can be created from this magical technique, which can be used for a wide variety of purposes. One is limited only by one's imagination as to what can be worked for with this method. Astrology will be found to be useful, as by using the colours, incenses and imagery of a planet complete rituals can be created for any working.

Vibratory Formula of the Middle Pillar

One technique that can be used for invocation and also for charging talismanic figures via the Middle Pillar is the Vibratory Formula. This is a method of working which is direct and simple and above all else effective. Firstly the LBRP will be performed, as will a general invocation. After the working of the Middle Pillar, the operator will need to visualise Kether as a brilliant sphere above their head. Next see in front of you the letters of the God Name of the Sephira that you are working with. If you can visualise them in their Hebrew lettering so much the better.

As you breathe in draw the letters into your body. Then imagine the bright light of Kether being drawn down and infusing the letters with power. The God Name can be silently intoned several times as a mantra so that you can feel your body vibrating with the energies that have been aroused. Raise both your hands so that they are both level with your ears, then throw them outwards with the first finger pointing out or at the object that is being charged and as you do so let the name and the energy pour out from you and into the direction that it is going. This must be done with utmost authority and all the force that you can muster. If a general invocation is being used imagine that the name is resonating throughout creation, but if you are charging an object let the object absorb the force that has been summoned and see it being sucked in to the object as it is projected outwards from you.

Sephirothic Imagery:

Each of the ten Sephiroth have a meditational image that can be built up and concentrated upon. When they are established, if you walk into the scene in your *'mind's eye'* the meditator can interact and experience the energies that they represent. Thus by names and images are great powers awoken. This technique which Jung called *'active imagination,'* can be used to explore the Kabbalistic realms. Other symbols that can be used with success are tarot card trumps. These are very effective and highly recommended to work with the energies of the twenty-two paths of the Tree as there is a card for each of the paths. This is also the same with the Hebrew letters, again there are twenty-two, one for each card and path that will allow ingress.

The magical imagery of the ten Sephiroth can also be built around one's self in meditation and one's consciousness can be placed within to experience and connect with the energy that it represents. This will need to be done under ritual conditions. Such rites can be built around the colours, incense and invocations that are relevant to the working.

Also the seals of the angels that are associated with each of the twenty-two paths can be accessed by visualising them as a door and entering therein. Again this will need to be done under ritual conditions; they can also be worked with via candle magic. This can be done by carving their seals on a candle, one that is preferably of their colour, as angels are of the worlds of Yetzirah that colour scheme should be used.

They can be worked with to bring into your life the energy that the path represents. This can sometimes be a disruptive experience but it is always instructive. The workings start with a wash or shower; this is done with the intent that all that which is negative to the working is stripped from your being. The working site, which can be a room specially set aside or a bedroom, will need to be cleaned and tidied.

A small table for an altar is placed in the middle of the working space and covered with a white cloth, although one that is coloured to suit the rite will be ideal but not always practicable. Place two candles upon the altar, these can be coloured white. Incense that is relevant to the working can be burnt. This is a useful aid as it will help induce a right frame of mind. A general invocation to God for the success of the working takes place, as does the invocation of the God Name and the Archangel for ingress into the Sephira that you are working with. If you are working one of the paths however you will need to invoke both the God Names and the Archangelic beings that preside over the Sephira at the beginning and the ending of the path in question. The whole technique of pathworking is well known to the occult student.

It will suffice to say that creating a mental landscape with the imagery and colours that relate to the path that you are working with, and then entering into it in an imaginative way, so that you are interacting with the scenes as they arise, will enable you to experience the energies of the path. When the working is finished, close the doorways and thank the names involved for their assistance.

Finish with the LBRP to close the rite and record your impression of the working, although if you are working in a group setting you may wish to discuss your experiences. It is not uncommon in such circumstances for all to have similar experiences and imagery occur. Interestingly, some of the imagery you may very well find cropping up in the following few days after each working has been performed. This I feel is a good thing, although it is unlikely that it will always happen for you. If it does then accept that the symbols and the working are stirring the deeps of your psyche and that you are tuning in to the energies of the Tree.

Another route of ingress which is more complex but worth studying is to create the temple of Malkuth and from there rise through each Sephira until you get to the path or sphere that you wish to experience. This work will start and end at Malkuth. If you are working in a room that is solely dedicated to your magic then the regular building up of the temple of Malkuth will be a very useful means to access the inner worlds and to bring their energies through to the everyday levels of existence.

The temple of Malkuth will have three doorways, as there are three paths arising out of Malkuth. By entering the relevant doorway and travelling the path until it gets to the next Sephira, the meditator can enter the temple of that Sephira. From here they can access the path to the next Sephira and subsequently work their way through the Tree, experiencing its energies and potentialities. The temples will form along the lines of their colours and symbolism.

By working this way a thorough grounding in the Western Mysteries can be experienced, and an initiation takes place on more than one level with this type of esoteric working; this will be beneficial in all your acts of magic as the symbols become part of the warp and weft of your psyche.

CHAPTER SIX

Rites and Rituals

The Temple of Malkuth

An altar will be needed in the centre of the working space that is covered with a white cloth. Upon this place two lighted white candles with no other lighting. Let the incense be something heavy like patchouli, or failing that, frankincense or church incense may be used as a general incense for all workings. Having washed, dress in a black robe with a hood as this will be useful. Primarily we are endeavouring to detach from the everyday world; this is symbolised by the robe and the hood which will shut out distractions when meditating upon the symbols used. Perform both the Kabbalistic Cross and LBRP as given earlier. Use a general invocation such as the one given below or write your own.

> *'Blessed art thou Lord of Creation*
> *Blessed art thou whom Nature hath not formed*
> *Blessed art thou God the Vast and Mighty One*
> *Thou who art Lord of the Light and the Darkness!'*

Declare your intent and invoke the names that govern the energies of Malkuth such as given below or again create your own invocations. Remember that the God Name is first then the archangel as we are going down through the four worlds, so there is a strict pecking order to follow.

> *'For in and by the holy Names of God ADONIA HA ARETZ*
> *Lord of this earth!*
> *And in the mighty name of the Archangel Sandalphon Let the angels of Malkuth*
> *Share with us the mysteries of the Kingdom!'*

After reading the Yetziratic text that is associated with Malkuth, seat yourself comfortably, and quietly relax. Let your mind go blank as you slow down your thoughts, this won't be easy as they keep breaking through like a chattering monkey! But persevere with this practice.

Now let the following imagery arise. With your eyes closed see the room become a holy temple. The floor is coloured black and white as a chess board. This is the pattern of the temple floor that Solomon built. In the middle will be seen the altar which is waist high and is the size of a cube placed upon another cube. This is covered with a white cloth on which will burn a lamp. On this altar will also be several ears of corn and fruits of the earth. In the east are two pillars, the one on the left is black and is severity. The pillar on the right is coloured white and is mercy. These are the two columns of the Tree of Life.

Beyond the pillars are three doors. Each of these has a curtain drawn over them to symbolise that they are closed. The middle doorway is the thirty-second path from Malkuth to Yesod. If it is being worked with then the tarot card The World will be seen as the door and the curtain drawn back. The door on the left is the thirty-first path to Hod and will display the tarot card Judgment if it is being worked with. The path on the right is to Netzach the twenty-ninth path. The tarot card will be The Moon. High on the eastern wall will be seen the figure of a winged man, on the southern wall will be seen the winged lion, on the west wall will be the eagle and on the north wall will be the winged bull. These are the signs that represent the elements.

By working with this imagery several times it will be built up quickly on the subtle levels, thus making contact easier each time. Experience the imagery and as you stand in the temple let the forces of Malkuth manifest around you. Sometimes this may become a fertile scene in a field or something else that will express the nature of Malkuth. If any people appear, it is always considered magical courteousness to let them start any conversation.

Sometimes you may pick up thoughts about the nature of the working or feelings about its nature. These thoughts can be difficult after the work is completed to express in words, as they seem to slip through your mind, but they do leave you with impressions as to what it is that you are being told.

Close the working by stamping your foot or rapping upon the altar top to emphasise that you are back in the everyday world. Give thanks to the names and energies for assisting you and for letting you explore their mysteries, followed by a general prayer of thanks to divinity for the working. Finish with the LBRP.

It is a useful exercise to write down any impressions that you have, however fleeting, to help earth the experience; also something to eat will be useful too. By following this format and by changing the names and colours you will be able to explore the Tree of Life and its energies.

If working with the twenty-two paths, there are various meditative approaches which can be taken; of these I will outline four. Firstly when working with a path one must invoke the energies of the Sephira at the beginning and ending of the path. This is done by first calling upon the energies of the Sephira from which the path starts and then the energies of the Sephira where the path ends. Also with the paths invoke the angel that presides over each of the paths. The angel will be the guide and will show the mysteries of the path.

The path can be worked by starting at Malkuth and travelling up the relevant path to the next Sephira. Here let the temple form which will be based upon the colour and symbols of the Sephira. In the temple will be the doors for the paths that precede therefrom. The path that you need for the next Sephira will have the relevant tarot card as the door through which one travels. This method can be used for travelling all over the Tree, starting with the thirty-second and working them in order. If you work one path a fortnight that will be sufficient as a little time will be needed for the energies to settle within the psyche. Other means of working the paths can simply be done by visualising the Tarot card as the doorway, after performing LBRP etc, and travelling through that. One can also use the seal of the angel as the doorway and visualise it drawn upon the door and travel through that.

The seal will have to be drawn in the Yetzirah colours relevant to the path, which have been given elsewhere. Also will be of use are the invocations which are from a traditional source which are associated with each of the Hebrew letters and therefore the angel and tarot card of each path.

Finally there is candle magic. This has been written upon elsewhere, (See Michael Howard's *'Candle Burning'* for more information). After inscribing the angel's seal upon a candle you can either see the imagery build up in the candle flame or place the candle in front of a mirror that is solely used for magic and skry into the mirror in an endeavour to contact the angel of the path. , It is best if the candle is a suitable colour for the working, but white will suffice, Again the usual preliminaries are to take place before the working.

This method is a good way to work with the angel if you want the energies of the path to manifest in your life to resolve an issue for you. Alternatively you can use the seal that has been drawn upon parchment: place this under the candle and see the angel working the magic in the flame or mirror as already suggested. The seal can become a talismanic figure of the working which must be kept safely.

In time the energies of the Tree of Life will become apparent in your life and as you explore the world of Western Occultism this will become more relevant for you as the mystery unfolds and experiences are had.

Therefore there becomes a blessed state whereby the individual moves from a belief in God to knowledge of God, a state that is not offered by religion. Having eaten of the fruit of the Tree of Life the eyes of man are open and he sees himself as he really is - God-like.

'For like can only be comprehended by like, for such is the mystery of God.'

Massa Aborum Vitae: The Mass of the Tree of Life

'And the Lord God said, Behold the man is become as one of us,
To know good and evil:
And now, lest he put forth his hand and take also of the tree of Life and eat,
and live for ever.'

This Mass, which comes from a working group who study, practice and work with the Magical Traditions of the West, will need some experience of the workings that have been given previously to get the best from it. Such workings are a religious/ceremonial art form, something which established religions have forgotten. Sounds, symbols and sacred drama can have an inspiring and dramatic effect on those who regularly participate in such events. This working can be adapted as one's sense of the art demands and nothing in its structure is dogmatic.

That which is in bold type is said or intoned by all. Let the altar be draped in white and dressed with white candles, and use Abra-Melin, frankincense or a general church incense as the suffumigation. The altar has a chalice of red wine in the centre on which rests a paten that holds enough bread for those who are partaking.

The Tree is built up in the mind over the altar, with Kether in the vast heights so that as it develops, Malkuth will be over the chalice. If you can visualise the paths as the tree is built up so much the better; this is the ideal for this working, even if they are in a white colour. However let the Sephira be in their Atziluth colours and if possible try to place even momentarily one's consciousness in each sphere as you are coming down the Tree. If you cannot manage the paths at this stage then simply come down on the lightening flash as shown. This represents the descent of power from Kether to Malkuth. Finally the Tree is visualised as being poured into the bread and wine, and then consumed by those present as a living talismanic experience. There will be no need for a banishing afterwards, just a simple prayer of thanks will suffice.

The Lightning Flash:

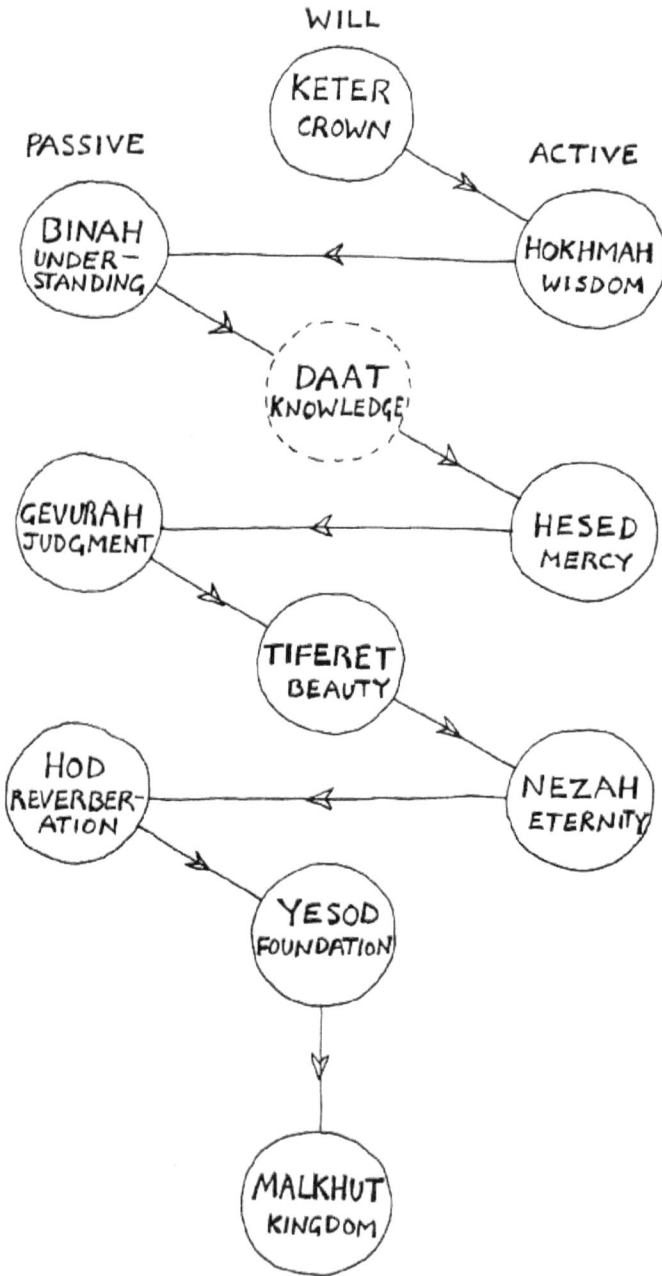

Otz Chim

Perform LBRP in the usual manner:

Celebrant:

> *Powers of the Kingdom, be ye beneath my left foot, be thou in my right hand!*
> *Glory and eternity touch my shoulders and guide me in the paths of victory.*
> *Mercy and justice be ye the equilibrium and splendour of my life.*
> *Understanding and wisdom give unto me the crown.*
> *Spirits of Malkuth conduct me between the two columns whereon is supported the whole edifice of the temple.*
> *Angels of Netzach and of Hod strengthen me upon the cubical stone of Yesod.*
> *O Gedulahel! O Geburahel! O Tipereth!*
> *Binael be thou my love!*
> *Ruach Chokmahael be thou my light*
> *Be that which thou art and that which thou willest to be*
> *O Ketheriel!*
> *Ishim assist me in the name of Shaddai Cherubim be my strength in the name Adonai.*
> *Beni Elohim be ye my brethren in the name of the son and by the virtues of Tzabaoth.*
> *Elohim fight for me in the name of YHVH*
> *Seraphim purify my love in the name of Eloah. Chaschmalim enlighten me with the splendours of Elohi and of Schechinah*
> *Aralim act ye; Auphanim revolve and shine.*
> *Chaioth Ha-Qadosch cry aloud speak roar and groan.*
> *Qadosch, Qadosch, Qadosch, Shaddai Adonai Yod Zchavah Eheieh Asher Eheieh!*
> *So Mote It Be!*

Introitus:

Celebrant:

> *Out of Nothing cometh All Unto which all things doth return*
> *So Mote It Be!*

All say:

> *Holy art thou Lord of Creation*
> *Holy art thou God of Mine Soul*
> *Holy art thou of whom I am*
> *For thou art Lord of both the Light and the Darkness and without thee nothing is!*

Credo:

All say:

> I believe in one Godhead who art the sum of all creation and is both male and female.
> Who created Heaven, Earth and Hell the Bright and the Dark
> that life may be expressed. Furthermore I confirm that I am of God and that there is no part of me that is not of God!
> Whereof creation is both within and without and that I am therefore but an expression thereof!
> For I declare that I am of God, loved by God, sustained by God created in the holy image
> unto whom all shall return.
> Therefore be steadfast and fear naught
> for virtue abideth not in the heart of the coward!
> Wherefore there is but one initiation and that is life
> and the experience thereof.
> And of that holy mystery of which I am
> Hear O Creation for the Lord is One! Dei Voco:

Celebrant:

> Behold the Tree and the great mystery thereof!

Celebrant: (Kether:)

> For Kether is the Crown
> EH- HEH –YEH
> and of Metatron thy Holy Archangel may the Chaoth Ha Qadesh
> The Holy Living Creatures
> grant unto us the Completion of the Great Work – The Attainment

(Chokmah:)

> For thine is the Wisdom
> YHVH
> Let the Archangel Ratziel and the Holy Angels the Auphanim and the Matzaloth – the Zodiac
> grant unto us the Vision of God Face to Face and the virtue of Devotion.

(Binah:)

> For thine is Understanding
> YHVH ELOHIM
> Let the Holy Angels the Aralim by the powers of Shabbati –Saturn

grant that we may receive the Vision of Sorrow
and the Devotion of Silence.

(Chesed:)

Unto thee is Love
EL
divine and wonderful
Let the Archangel Tzadkiel and the Holy angels the Chasmalim by
the power of Tzedek – Jupiter
grant unto us the Vision of Love and the Virtue of Obedience

(Geburah:)

Unto thee be the power
ELOHIM GIBOR
Let thine Archangel Khamael and the Holy Seraphim
by the power of Madim – Mars
grant unto us the Vision of Power and the Virtue of Courage

(Tiphereth:)

Unto thee be the Beauty and Harmony
YHVH ALOAH VA DAATH
God made manifest in the sphere of the mind
Let thine Archangel Mikael and the Malachim
by the powers of Shemesh – the Sun
grant unto us the Vision of the Harmony of all Things and the Devotion to the Great Work

(Netzach:)

Unto thee be the Victory
YHVH TZABAOTH
Lord of Armies art thou
Let thine Archangel Haniel and the Holy Elohim
by the power of Nogah – Venus
grant unto us the Vision of Beauty Triumphant and the Virtue of Unselfishness

(Hod:)

Unto thee be the Glory and the Splendour
ELOHIM TZABAOTH
God of Hosts
Let thine Archangel Raphael and the Holy Beni Elohim
by the power of Kokab – Mercury

> grant unto us the Vision of Glory Triumphant
> And the Virtue of Truthfulness

(Yesod:)

> Unto thee be the foundation
> SHADDAI EL CHAI
> Almighty Living God
> Let thine Archangel Gabriel
> and the Holy Ashim
> by the power of Levanah - the Moon
> grant unto us the Vision of The Machinery of the Universe The Treasure House of Images and the Virtue of Independence

(Malkuth:)

> Unto thee be the Kingdom
> ADONAI HA ARETZ
> Lord of this Earth
> Let thine Archangel Sandalphon and the Holy Kerubim
> by the power of the Four Elements
> grant unto us the Vision of the Holy Guardian Angel and the Virtue of Discrimination

All visualise the Tree pouring into the bread and the wine as the following is said by the celebrant:

> For in and by the Holy Names of God and the ten stations of the descending light let this bread and this wine be consecrated unto our bodies that it may make for health, wealth, strength and joy of spirit So Mote It Be!

Consume and share:

Now concentrate on Kether above your head and momentarily place one's consciousness therein. Whilst doing this intone the following invocation as you see your auric field glowing and being charged with the powers of creation.

> 'I am he the bornless spirit
> having sight in the feet strong and the immortal fire!
> I am he the truth
> I am he who hates that evil shall be wrought in the world
> I am he who lighteneth and thundereth
> I am he from whom is the shower of the life on earth I am he the begetter and the manifestor
> unto the light

The heart girt with a serpent is my name!
Come thou forth and follow me and make all spirits subject unto me so that every spirit of the firmament
and of the ether upon earth
and on dry land, or in the water, of whirling air or of rushing fire
and every spell of God the Vast and Mighty One may be obedient unto me!
IAO SABAO
Such are the words!

Close by giving thanks in your own wording.

*'It is I who hath planted this Tree So that the world may gaze At it in wonder.
With it I have encompassed the All and have named it the All.
All things depend upon it Look upon it and yearn for it
and from it all souls doth proceed and all souls must return.'*

Further Reading

Halevi, Z'ev ben Shimon (1989) *Adam and the Kabbalistic Tree.* Red Wheel-Weiser, Maine

Highfield, A.C (1984) *The Book of Celestial Images.* Harper Collins, London

Kaplan, Aryeh 1997() *Sefer Yetzirah.* Weiser Books, Maine

Rankine, David (2005) *Climbing the Tree of Life.* Avalonia, London

Rankine, David & d'Este, Sorita (2009) *Practical Qabalah Magick.* Avalonia, London

Regardie, Israel (2002) *The Middle Pillar.* Llewellyn, Minnesota

Regardie, Israel (1995) *A Garden of Pomegranates.* Llewellyn, Minnesota

Index

A

Abra-Melin 34, 111
Adam Kadmon 13
Aiah 49, 50, 82, 83
Ain Soph 16
air 24, 40, 46, 47, 50, 99, 117
Aleph 49, 50, 98
aloes 42
amber 34, 37, 65, 90
ambergris ..21, 25, 27, 30, 32, 34, 37
Aquarius 24, 46, 86, 99
Aralim 27, 28, 113, 114
Archangel .18, 26, 28, 31, 33, 35, 38, 40, 43, 45, 107
Aries 59, 60
Ashim 44, 45, 116
Assiah ..13, 15, 19, 22, 24, 44, 49, 51, 53, 56, 59, 61, 63, 65, 67, 69, 71, 73, 75, 77, 79, 82, 84, 86, 88, 90, 93, 95
Atziluth 13, 14, 18, 44, 49, 51, 53, 56, 59, 61, 63, 65, 67, 69, 71, 73, 75, 77, 79, 82, 84, 86, 90, 93, 95, 111
Auphanim 25, 26, 113, 114
Ayin 82, 83
azure 30

B

Bachour 51
Beni Elohim 39, 40
benzoin 37
Beth 51, 52
Biah 51, 52
Binah ...27, 28, 29, 32, 44, 51, 56, 57, 63, 65, 114
black 27, 39, 44, 82, 95, 107, 108
blue 25, 30, 49, 53, 56, 71, 73, 75, 77, 79, 82, 86, 95, 99
Briah 13, 14, 18, 44, 49, 51, 53, 56, 59, 61, 63, 65, 67, 69, 71, 73, 75, 77, 79, 82, 84, 86, 88, 90, 93
brown 61, 65, 77, 88

C

camphor 53
Cancer 65
Capricorn 82
caraway 39
cassia 79
cedar 30, 71
Chaioth ha Qadesh 21
chalice. 27, 51, 53, 56, 59, 63, 65, 71, 75, 77, 79, 82, 84, 86, 88, 90, 95, 111
Chasmalim 30, 31, 115
Chazchazit 51, 52
Chesed 30, 31, 33, 61, 66, 67, 69, 71, 115
Cheth 65, 66
Chiah 14, 65, 66
Chokmah ..25, 26, 28, 32, 47, 49,

56, 57, 59, 61, 114
cinnamon 34, 90
citrine 42, 44
civet 27
copal 93
crimson 27, 88, 93

D

Daath ... 17, 34, 53, 59, 63, 69, 73, 77, 79, 82, 102
dagger 77, 86, 88
Dagoul 56
Daleth 56, 57
Dark Night of the Soul 54, 80
Diah 56, 57
Djinn 46
dragons blood 32, 59
Dweller on the Threshold 54

E

earth 17, 24, 35, 45, 46, 47, 55, 62, 66, 72, 73, 74, 81, 97, 99, 107, 108, 109, 116, 117
Ecclesiastes 12
6   45
Eden 11, 45
Ehieh 21, 49
elfhame 87
Elohim . 27, 32, 37, 38, 39, 40, 50, 51, 52, 55, 56, 57, 60, 62, 63, 64, 65, 66, 67, 68, 70, 72, 73, 74, 75, 76, 78, 80, 82, 83, 84, 85, 87, 89, 90, 93, 94, 96, 102, 113, 115
emerald 37, 49, 56, 73

F

fennel 39
fire . 15, 24, 35, 40, 44, 46, 47, 60, 93, 94, 99, 116, 117
frankincense 34, 67, 90, 93, 107, 111

G

Gabriel 42, 43, 79, 86, 90, 95, 99, 116
Gadol 55
galbanum 49, 73, 86
Geburah 32, 33, 65, 67, 73, 75, 98, 115
Gedulah .... 30, 31, 39, 98, See Chesed
Gemini 63, 64
Genesis 3
226
Ghob 46
Giah 53, 54
Gimel 53, 55
gnomes 46
God Name 18, 19, 22, 33, 38, 44, 56, 59, 61, 63, 65, 67, 69, 71, 73, 75, 77, 79, 82, 84, 86, 88, 90, 93, 95, 100, 102, 103, 105, 107
gold 22, 24, 35, 37, 44, 54, 68, 83, 93
Golden Dawn 98
Great Bear 38
green ... 37, 49, 56, 67, 69, 73, 75, 77, 79, 84, 89
grey 25, 27, 51, 63, 67, 69, 82
Guph 15

H

Hadom 59
Haniel .. 37, 38, 71, 77, 84, 86, 88, 115
Hasid 65
Hazaz 82, 83
Heh 14, 15, 46, 59, 60, 99, 102
Hiah 59, 60
Hod 39, 40, 41, 75, 82, 84, 85, 90, 93, 108, 113, 115
Holy Graal 87

I

Iah 69
Iiah 69, 70
Inanna 11
indigo 42, 51, 61, 77, 82, 95

J

jasmine 42
Jupiter 30, 31, 71, 115

K

Kabbalistic Cross 98, 99
Kabir 71, 72
Kadosh 88, 89
Kaph 71, 72
Kerubim 42, 43, 116
Kether .. 12, 17, 21, 22, 24, 25, 30, 44, 47, 49, 51, 53, 54, 68, 103, 111, 114, 116
Khamael 32, 33, 65, 67, 73, 75, 115
Kiah 71, 72
Kokab .... See Mercury

L

Lamed 73, 74
lamp 37, 38, 56, 69, 71, 93
lavender 39
Leo 24, 46, 67, 99
Lesser Banishing Ritual of the Pentagram .... 97, See LBRP
Levanah .... See Moon
Levi, Eliphas 98
Liah 73, 74
Liber Noctis 100
Libra 73
Lightning Flash 68, 73, 112
Limmud 73
lotus 65
Lucifer 38, 87

M

Macrocosm 13
Madim .... See Mars
Malachim 34, 35, 115
Malkuth 12, 43, 44, 45, 47, 68, 78, 88, 93, 95, 98, 102, 105, 107, 108, 109, 111, 113, 116
maroon 65
Mars 32, 33, 60, 84, 115
Masloth 25
mastic 51
Mathers, MacGregor 98
mauve 63, 86
Meborak 75
Mem 75, 76, 98
Mercury 39, 40, 51, 115
Metatron . 21, 22, 49, 51, 53, 114
Miah 75, 76
Microcosm 13
Middle Pillar 97, 100, 102, 103
Mikael.. 34, 35, 40, 53, 59, 63, 69, 77, 79, 82, 99, 115
mirror 75
Moon 42, 43, 53, 88, 108, 116
Morning Star 38
musk 82
myrrh 27, 75, 79
myrtle 56

N

Nephesch 14
Neschamah 14
Netzach 37, 38, 40, 71, 77, 84, 85, 86, 87, 88, 89, 108, 113, 115
Niah 77, 78
Niksa 46
Nogah .... See Venus
Nora 77
Nun 77, 78, 98

O

olive 37, 44, 61, 75, 86
opoponax 77
orange 39, 59, 61, 63, 90, 93

P

Paralda 46
patchouli 44, 107
Path of the Arrow 54
Peh 84, 85
pentacle 49, 51, 61, 71, 84, 88, 90, 93, 95
pepper 84
Phodeh 84, 85
Piah 84, 85
pink 27, 34, 88, 102
Pisces 88
plum 69
Primum Mobile 21, 24
Proverbs 3 17-18 17
purple ... 30, 39, 51, 67, 71, 75, 86

Q

Qoph 88, 89
Quiah 88, 89

R

Rankine, David 99
Raphael 35, 39, 40, 75, 82, 84, 90, 93, 99, 115
Rashith ha Gilgalim 21
Ratziel 25, 26, 49, 56, 59, 61, 114
red . 25, 33, 39, 59, 61, 67, 84, 89, 90, 99, 111
red sandalwood 37
Regardie, Israel 99
Resh 90, 92, 94
Riah 90, 91
Rodeh 90
Rosa Mystica 37
rose 32, 33, 34, 36, 37, 38, 56, 71

russet 39, 44, 65

S

Sagittarius 79
salamanders 46
Samekh 79, 80
Sandalphon 44, 45, 88, 93, 95, 107, 116
Saturn 27, 28, 95, 114
scarlet 59, 84, 93
Scorpio 24, 46, 77, 78, 99
Sepher Yetzirah 19
Sephira 16, 17, 18, 19, 20, 25, 26, 28, 30, 33, 35, 38, 40, 42, 43, 44, 47, 68, 103, 105, 109, 111, See Sephiroth
Sephiroth .. 13, 16, 17, 18, 19, 98, 104
Seraphim 32, 33, 113, 115
Shaddai 42, 79, 86, 88, 90, 93, 94, 95, 102, 113
Shekinah 17, 55
Shemesh .... See Sun
Shiah 93, 94
Shin 93
Siah 79, 80
silver 53, 54
Somek 79, 80
spear 73, 79
storax 44, 61, 95
Sun 15, 34, 35, 40, 80, 86, 90, 91, 93, 115
sword .. 32, 33, 51, 59, 63, 65, 67, 73, 84
sylphs 46

T

Tarot 20, 24, 47, 49, 51, 53, 56, 59, 61, 63, 65, 67, 69, 71, 73, 75, 77, 79, 82, 84, 86, 88, 90, 93, 95, 109
Tau 47, 95, 96

Index

Taurus 24, 46, 61, 99
Tehod 67
Teth 67, 68
Tetragrammaton 46
Thechinah 95
Thiah 95, 96
Tiah 67, 68
Tiphereth ..34, 35, 40, 53, 54, 59, 63, 69, 73, 77, 78, 79, 80, 82, 83, 115
Transcendental Magic 98
Treasure House of Images 43, 116
Tzaddi 86, 87
Tzadkiel 30, 31, 61, 67, 69, 71, 115
Tzaphkiel 27, 28, 51, 56, 63, 65
Tzedek ... 86, 87, 115, See Jupiter
Tziah 86, 87

U
undines 46

V
Vau 61, 62
Venus 37, 38, 56, 57, 115
vermillion 93
Vezio 61
Viah 61, 62
Vibratory Formula 103
violet 30, 39, 42, 51, 71, 86
Virgo 69

W
wand 49, 51, 53, 56, 61, 63, 67, 69, 75, 82, 90, 93
water ... 24, 43, 46, 47, 59, 75, 76, 99, 117
white ... 22, 24, 25, 33, 39, 75, 86, 88, 99, 105, 107, 108, 109, 111
white sandalwood 42
wormwood 63

Y
Yechidah 14
yellow .. 25, 30, 34, 42, 44, 49, 51, 63, 67, 71, 79, 90, 99, 102
Yesod ... 42, 43, 47, 79, 86, 87, 90, 91, 95, 108, 113, 116
Yetzirah 13, 14, 19, 44, 49, 51, 53, 56, 59, 61, 63, 65, 67, 69, 71, 73, 75, 77, 79, 82, 84, 86, 88, 90, 93, 95, 104, 109
Yod 14, 25, 46, 69, 70, 99, 113

Z
Zain 63, 64
Zakai 63, 64
Ziah 63, 64
Zodiac . 25, 26, 59, 61, 63, 65, 67, 69, 71, 73, 75, 77, 79, 82, 84, 86, 88, 90, 95, 114
Zohar 12, 13, 31

FOUNDATIONS OF PRACTICAL SORCERY

A seven-volume set of magical treatises, unabridged, comprising:

Vol. I - Liber Noctis

A Handbook of the Sorcerous Arte

Liber Noctis explores the attitudes, training and preparation required for success in ritual, and, as the title suggests, does not shy away from the 'darker' aspects of magic. Practical, experiential, lucid and non-judgmental, this book lays the groundwork for the successful study and practice of sorcery in the modern world.

Vol. II - Ars Salomonis

Being of that Hidden Arte of Solomon the King

Ars Salomonis is a practical manual for working with the talismanic figures found in the Key of Solomon, the most significant of all grimoires. Including two methods for empowering and activating the planetary pentacles, the author makes this vital work safely accessible to beginners. It is an ideal entranceway into the grimoire tradition.

Vol. III - Ars Geomantica

Being an account and rendition of the Arte of Geomantic Divination and Magic

Ars Geomantica explores the medieval system of Geomancy, one of the simplest and most practical of the divinatory arts. The inclusion of detailed instructions on the creation of geomantic staves, elemental fluid condensers, and talismanic construction and consecration make this work a superb introduction to an extensive assortment of magical and divinatory principles.

Vol. IV - Ars Theurgia Goetia

Being an account and rendition of the Arte and Praxis of the Conjuration of some of the Spirits of Solomon

Ars Theurgia Goetia presents a precise and practical guide to working with the spirits of this neglected text from the Solomonic grimoire cycle, the Theurgia-Goetia, giving the full seals of the spirits for the first time. The complete ritual sequence of preparation, conjuration, and license to depart is lucidly demonstrated, making this work suitable for both the beginner and the experienced practitioner.

Vol. V - Otz Chim

The Tree of Life

Otz Chim is a practical exploration of the magic of the Kabbalistic Tree of Life, the glyph that concentrates the essence of magic and mysticism within the Western Mystery Tradition. This book focuses on lesser-known aspects such as the angels associated with the paths, their seals, and invocations and includes the previously unavailable Massa Aborum Vitae.

Vol. VI - Ars Speculum

Being an Instruction on the Arte of using Mirrors and Shewstones in Magic

Ars Speculum is a concise and practical work on the use of mirrors and shewstones in magic. In it the author explores skrying and working with the four elements of air, fire, water and earth - both with elemental condensers and different elemental creatures. Other techniques include contacting other levels of being, the conjuration of spirits, binding and ligature, and healing and protection.

Vol. VII - Liber Terriblis

Being an Instruction on the seventy-two Spirits of the Goetia

Liber Terribilis is a practical study of how to work with the seventy-two spirits of the infamous seventeenth-century Grimoire, the Goetia. It also explores the vital and often neglected use of the seventy-two binding angels of the Great Name of God, the Schemhamphorasch. This volume will be of value to all levels of students and practitioners of the grimoire traditions, being based upon the work of a small group of occultists who have explored it in practice.

More information available on the Avalonia website-
www.avaloniabooks.co.uk

Or write to:
BM Avalonia
London
WC1N 3XX
England, United Kingdom

Gary St. M. Nottingham

Expanding the Esoteric Horizons ...

Avalonia is an independent publisher producing outstanding and innovative books which push the boundaries of their subjects and illuminate the spirit of the sacred in its many manifestations.

Explore some of the other works on the occult, mythology and magic published by Avalonia at:

www.avaloniabooks.co.uk

Readers who found Foundations of Practical Sorcery of interest, is likely to enjoy:

A Collection of Magical Secrets & a Treatise of mixed Cabalah by Stephen Skinner and David Rankine

Climbing the Tree of Life by David Rankine

Living Theurgy by Jeffrey S. Kupperman

Practical Elemental Magick by Sorita d'Este and David Rankine

The Book of Gold by David Rankine & Paul Harry Barron (trans.)

The Book of Treasure Spirits, edited by David Rankine

The Complete Grimoire of Pope Honorius by David Rankine & Paul Harry Barron (trans.)

The Cunning Man's Handbook by Jim Baker

The Grimoire of Arthur Gauntlet by David Rankine

Thoth by Lesley Jackson

Thracian Magic by Georgi Mishev

Wicca Magickal Beginnings by Sorita d'Este and David Rankine

www.ingramcontent.com/pod-product-compliance
Ingram Content Group UK Ltd.
Pitfield, Milton Keynes, MK11 3LW, UK
UKHW041259180426
11947UKWH00008B/565